New Facts
and
Old Families

From the Records of Frederick County, Maryland

NEW FACTS
and
OLD FAMILIES

From the Records of Frederick County, Maryland

By Millard Milburn Rice

With an Introduction by
Judge Edward S. Delaplaine,
Associate Justice, Maryland Court of Appeals (Ret.)

CLEARFIELD

Reprinted for
Clearfield Company, Inc. by
Genealogical Publishing Co., Inc.
Baltimore, Maryland
2002

INTRODUCTION

By Edward S. Delaplaine

Maryland has been very fortunate in having a long list of citizens who have become so fond of the history of their state that they have enjoyed spending many years in research, the results of which have helped greatly to preserve our heritage.

One native of Maryland who has found great enjoyment in the study of our history is Millard Milburn Rice. His roots in Maryland are deep. He was born in the town of Jefferson in Frederick County on September 19, 1894, the only child of Milton G. and Maria Culler Rice.

After graduating from Jefferson High School in 1910 and the Boys' High School of Frederick in 1912 he found his first employment in the Citizens National Bank in Frederick. In 1917 he entered Western Maryland College, but left in January 1918 to enlist in the United States Air Service. On September 17, 1919 he married Miss Mabel D. Long of Clarksburg, West Virginia. Their happy life together was terminated by her death on March 14, 1975. They had one son, Robert C. Rice, now a resident in Orlando, Florida.

Because of an ailment contracted in the service, Mr. Rice moved to Colorado for his health. There he spent fifteen years, during which time he wrote a number of articles on business, economic and political subjects for publication in leading periodicals. In 1935, his health having been restored, he returned from Colorado and for a time was engaged in dissemination of research for the Brookings Institution in Washington.

In December 1940 he returned to banking after an absence of twenty-five years. Until 1949 he served as Cashier and member of the Board of Directors of the

Woodbine National Bank; then from 1949 to 1963 he served as Executive Vice President and member of the Board of Directors of the Walkersville Bank. In 1963 when the Walkersville Bank was merged into the Farmers and Mechanics National Bank of Frederick, he was elected Vice President of the latter in charge of the Walkersville Office. He retired from that position in 1967, but continued as a member of the Advisory Board of the Walkersville Office.

For upwards of a decade thereafter he has had opportunity to enjoy historical and genealogical research. This book presents the fruits of his research.

It is apparent that the author derived particular enjoyment from his adventures in genealogy. His most ambitious effort dealt with the descendants of Jacob Koller (Culler), the Elder. He admits that he has been disappointed in not being able to discover Jacob's origins and what he did prior to the year 1750 when his name first appeared in the records of Frederick County. He also admits that the research was tedious because of the problems arising from the great number of variations in spelling of the names of descendants. Because of his painstaking efforts, this book will be of special value to descendants who wish to apply for membership in lineage societies such as the Daughters of the American Revolution, the Sons of the American Revolution, and the Society of the War of 1812.

While delving in the land records of Frederick County, Mr. Rice found an unusual coincidence: one of his great-great-grandfathers, Michael Culler, was the owner of a portion of a tract of land while the other portion was owned by another great-great-grandfather, George Baltus Dutrow. The discovery of this coincidence encouraged him to search for the descendants of the latter. Here again he ran into many difficulties and once more found innumerable variations in the spelling of names. But he persevered and he has given us the benefit of his painstaking research.

From genealogical research he turned to the study of the history of the town of Jefferson. That was natural for him, for not only is he a native of Jefferson, but he is a great-grandson of Henry Culler, who served as the town's first mayor. He points out that Jefferson was formed by joining two platted towns — New Town and New Freedom. This union was cemented by the Legislature of Maryland in an Act signed into law in 1832 by Governor George Howard.

Mr. Rice then became interested in Middletown, for Middletown and Jefferson have been friendly neighbors in lovely Middletown Valley. He describes the early years of Middletown and from his own research tells why he claims the version of the laying out of Middletown as told in the Histories of Western Maryland and of Frederick County is incorrect.

He then moves on to the town of Walkersville. The genesis of the town of Jefferson and Walkersville, the author emphasizes, were alike in one respect, but quite unlike in another. Each was a union of two villages, the town of Walkersville having been a combination of the village of Walkersville and the village of Georgetown. But, in contrast to Jefferson, neither Walkersville nor Georgetown was ever platted. "It just grew," he says.

Concerning the town called Monocacy, we meet with an unusual amount of controversy. Mr. Rice agrees with Dr. Abdel Ross Wentz that the community of Monocacy was not a platted town, but was instead a "string of plantations stretching more than ten miles down the Monocacy River, along the Carroll Creek, and on towards the Potomac."

Mr. Rice gives special attention to the controversy that has grown up over the first church in Monocacy. For some years it had been supposed that the old Moocacy Church had been built in 1732 along the Woodsboro-Creagerstown road. That supposition was rejected several years ago.

This book pays a tribute — richly deserved — to the Rev. David Candler, the Lutheran pastor who had charge of the parishes covering a wide area between the Susquehanna and the Potomac and under whose auspices the old church was built in 1743.

Considerable research had led Mr. Rice to the conclusion that Pastor Candler's church was located near Jimtown Crossroads — the intersection of Moser, Jimtown and Hessong Bridge Roads — probably near the old Eicholtz Mill.

Mr. Rice also presents his views on the controversial subject of the Frederick residence of John Hanson, who was often called the first President of the United States. After examining the land records of John Hanson and the will of Dr. Philip Thomas, Hanson's son-in-law, he has come to the conclusion that Hanson probably resided between the years 1772 and 1783 in a small dwelling that stood on the site of the house at 108 West Patrick Street.

We are indebted to the author for the fruits of his researches. They are entitled to respectful consideration.

NEW FACTS AND OLD FAMILIES
From the Records of Frederick County, Maryland

TABLE OF CONTENTS

PREFACE

The sketches in this book were researched and written over a period of twenty or more years, and there is nothing to be gained by an explanation of the reasons for their variety of subject matter. It is sufficient to say that the reasons are as varied as that subject matter!

While the research for the sketches is mine except where credit is indicated, they reach publication through Mr. John P. Dern, 950 Palomar Drive, Redwood City, California. In addition to extensive editorial encouragement and advice, he prepared the final manuscript for publication. Without his work this book would not exist.

In varying degrees I am indebted to many others, all too numerous to mention individually. This is to express to them my gratitude for their assistance.

In preparing these sketches for publication I have found and corrected several errors in earlier versions. This brings to mind a statement by the distinguished historian, Will Durant. After spending the greater part of his life writing history, he wrote a final little book, "Lessons of History." In it he said, "Most history is guessing and the rest is prejudice." My own very limited experience bears out this statement. I think it is almost impossible to write any history completely free of errors. It is my hope, however, that there are not too many in the sketches which follow.

MILLARD MILBURN RICE
116 Brooklawn Apartments
Frederick, Maryland 21701

RANDOM NOTES

In searching through the Land and Will Records of Frederick County, Maryland, as I worked on the little essays which follow, I have been intrigued by what one can learn of the interesting customs of ordinary people from earlier days.

Consider, for instance, the form and substance of wills. Without actual tabulation, I think it can be said that the majority of early wills probated before about 1820 were made on death-beds. Evidence of this is the brief interval between date of the will and date of probate. Many wills recite that the maker is "in a low and weak state of health, but of sound and disposing mind, memory and understanding."

This affirmation of soundness of "mind, memory and understanding" was most important, for the validity of the will depended upon it. When the will was probated, the three witnesses were required to appear before the Register of Wills and make affidavit that they saw the deceased sign and that they believed him to be competent.

Following the opening declaration of competence, most testators continued somewhat as follows: "Considering the certainty of Death and the uncertainty of the time thereof, to be prepared to leave this world when it shall please God to call me hence, I therefore make and publish this my last will and testament, that is to say, First and Principally, I commit my soul into the hands of Almighty God and my body to the earth...."

Frequently the provisions of a will disclose a great deal about family relationships. There may be a son

1

cut off with "five shillings sterling and no more." Or a married daughter's legacy may be directed to be retained and invested by an executor, the obvious purpose being to keep it out of the hands of the son-in-law.

Some of the provisions for the testators' widows seem strange. A widow's right of dower under English Common Law, which prevailed almost unchanged in the American Colonies, gave her a life-interest in one-third of her husband's real estate. But some of the provisions of husbands' wills seem almost designed to defeat this right. With provisions like the following in a will, the widow's future seems somewhat clouded:

After dividing his land equally between three sons, a man gives one son's part to his widow for life. Then he continues, "I give to my beloved wife the use of the dwelling house for twelve months after my decease, the use of half the garden for six years after my decease; and I devise that the Tobacco House and Orchard shall be for the use of my wife and all my children in common for the term of six years after my decease." Where does the widow live after twelve months, and what does she do for fruits and vegetables after six years?

In contrast to these Spartan conditions, some men made elaborately detailed provisions for a wife "so long as she remains unmarried." They left their farm lands to one or more sons, but directed that the widow should occupy the dwelling house, should have a cow of her choice and sometimes also a riding horse and side-saddle. Further, the sons must furnish their mother each year specified amounts of firewood, hay, corn, wheat, hackled flax, meat (generally pork), potatoes and sometimes cash and other items as well. Occasionally the sons' land titles were made contingent upon their compliance.

Until comparatively modern times a married woman in Maryland had no legal rights, other than her right of dower, which her husband was bound to respect. Almost literally she was the legal chattel of her husband. Frequently, if a married daughter re-

2

ceived a legacy under her father's will, it was paid to her husband, and there are instances found in the release records where a husband signed the release for his wife's legacy.

When a married man sold real estate, it was of course necessary for his wife to release her right of dower to the tract being sold. Otherwise the purchaser's title would not be clear. Apparently there were some wives who were reluctant to release their dower rights and also some husbands who, in some cases, resorted to physical violence to force their wives to acquiesce.

Until well into the Nineteenth Century, only a very few Frederick County wives signed deeds jointly with their husbands. They released their dower rights by special affidavit. At the bottom of the deed, or on its back, an affidavit by the husband, taken in Colonial days before "two of His Lordship's Justices" and later before two Justices of the Peace (or occasionally before the Clerk of Court and a deputy), reaffirmed ownership and the intention to transfer clear title to the purchaser.

To this was added a release of dower, of which the following is typical: "At the same time came Mary Doe, wife of the said John Doe whose name is signed to the aforegoing deed, and acknowledged that she freely relinquished her right of dower of and unto the said lands and premises within mentioned, and that she was not induced thereto by threats or fear of ill-usage from her husband or fear of his displeasure, she being by us privately examined out of the hearing of her husband...."

One occasional variation of the wife's affidavit is somewhat unusual. It merely recites something like "....and at the same time came Mary Doe, wife of John Doe, and acknowledged the foregoing instrument to be her act and deed." There would be nothing unusual in such an affidavit if made today, since this is the approximate modern form of affidavit when a wife joins in the deed and signs her name thereto. But when this affidavit refers to a deed in which the wife's name does not appear and which she did not sign, one wonders how she could call this her "act and deed."

In connection with the discussion of a married woman's legal rights and her rights of dower, it should be noted that beginning about the 1850s these rights began to be enlarged by numerous acts of the Maryland Legislature, and effective January 1, 1970 the rights of dower and curtesy were abolished. (Curtesy was the opposite of dower and was the husband's right under the Common Law to a life-estate in his deceased wife's real estate.) Statutory provisions now replace the Common Law in these matters.

Obviously there are numerous other interesting things found in the Frederick Land Records. Two in particular deserve special mention: the many changes in boundary lines resulting from resurveys and resurveys on resurveys, and the intriguing names given land grants and resurveys thereon.

As I note in the study of the Plat of Middletown, [1] there have been so many surveys and resurveys, claims and counter-claims in and around that town that the layman — and I suspect the surveyor also — is completely confused by them.

That part of the Town of Jefferson west of the Old Middletown Road, which was originally called New Freedom, was laid out on a tract of the same name. [2] That tract involved surveys and resurveys, all of which produce different boundary lines. For the same reason that people solve jig-saw puzzles I have made considerable effort to understand these differences.

Since NEW FREEDOM, in this particular example, was a resurvey on part of CHILDREN'S CHANCE, I reach the conclusion that the differences arise from the original survey of CHILDREN'S CHANCE made by Thomas Cresap for Isaac Wells in 1744. Cresap de-

---

[1] See below, p. 138.
[2] Ibid., pp. 31-35.

scribed his starting point as an "oak tree standing....
<u>at or near</u> the end of the First Line of.... LOW LAND"
which lay east of CHILDREN'S CHANCE.   Later surveys indicate that the tree didn't stand <u>at</u> the end of the
line and hence created a vacancy.   That was not the
only difference involved, but I think it obviously contributed to the others.

Elias DeLashmutt, Jr., laid out the Town of New
Freedom about 1795, but the last resurvey on the tract
NEW FREEDOM was made seven years later.   I think
this resurvey showed that the western part of his town
encroached on land he didn't own.   Proof of this is evidenced by the 1832 plat of Jefferson,[3] whereon are
shown foreshortened lots on the south side of the street
at the west end.

When Pullman cars were more in vogue than they
are today, there were numerous jokes about the out-
landish and exotic names assigned to both Pullman
cars and race horses.   The same humor may be evident in the names given tracts of land in Frederick
County.   Names of the many hundreds of such tracts
range from the sublime to the ridiculous.   Some are
self-explanatory, some so odd they seem meaningless.

DEN OF WOLVES, near Creagerstown, quite
probably indicates that when it was first surveyed in
1742 there was a wolf den on it.   That seems to tell its
own story, as does CATCH AS CATCH CAN, HE
WHO GETS THE LAND IS THE BEST MAN, located
about two miles north of Jefferson.   Likewise, perhaps, the tract END OF STRIFE, near Myersville.

But there are endless implications in the tract
name BITE HIM SOFTLY.   And one near Lewistown
so intrigued me that I traced it to its origin.   I wonder
what scholar translated BONE HIM, SECURE HIM
from its Latin original of BONUM SECURUM!

---

[3] Ibid., pp. 38-39.

5

THE MONOCACY QUAKER MEETING HOUSE SITE

The first building for religious worship erected in Maryland west of the Monocacy River was the Monocacy Quaker Meeting House. Built in 1738-39, it antedated by four or five years the first Lutheran Church (1743) and by approximately eight years the first chapel of the Church of England.[1]

But for at least a century the site of this first building has not been pinpointed, and the Quaker organization within whose supervisory territory it lies had little or no knowledge of it. This is true in spite of the fact that, unless lost through adverse possession, the Quaker Burying Ground near the church site is still Quaker property within which are buried several pioneer members of the Monocacy Meeting.

Modern historians, by a process of logic, have assumed that the Quaker Meeting House was built on a tract of land called JOSIAH, which was originally granted in 1725 to Josiah Ballenger, in whose house the Quakers first met.

Heretofore, the only clue to the location of the Meeting House was that it was built "near Josiah Ballenger's house." Hence the logical conclusion that it was on JOSIAH, which would place it east northeast of present-day Buckeystown, Maryland.

Through a recently-discovered clue, I find that it was built about four-tenths of a mile west of Buckeys-

---

[1] Dr. Grace L. Tracey, Notes from the Records of Old Monocacy (mss., Hampstead, Md., copyright 1958), p. 218.

6

town, and the following text and plats are presented as proof.

On March 27, 1731 a survey of 400 acres, called GOOD LUCK, was made for Meredith Davis, a Quaker from lower Prince George's County.[2] On April 27, 1739 Davis conveyed five acres of GOOD LUCK to two members of the Monocacy Meeting as trustees.[3] The Meeting had been established in 1726 by authority of the New Garden Monthly Meeting of Chester County, Pennsylvania.[4]

The deed to the trustees, William Matthews and Henry Ballenger, described the five-acre tract as beginning "at a.....tree standing on the north side of a meadow and at the head of a spring." The courses and distances of the tract from the point of beginning were:

SE x S 40 perches
NE x N 20 perches
NW x N 40 perches
Straight line to Beginning

However, these courses and distances produce a parallelogram of less than five acres, although in every recorded transaction thus far found, the tract is treated as containing exactly five acres.[5] This raises the question as to just what were the exact courses and distances — a question of extreme importance in undertaking to locate the Quaker Burying Ground, since its beginning point was tied to the end of the second line of the five-acre tract.

The deed itself is apparently lost. Could it be that the original Prince George's County copyist erred and subsequent copies compound that error? Did Meredith Davis, in his original deed, intend to "box the

---

[2] Ibid., p. 56. See below, p. 15.
[3] Frederick County Land Records, WR 10-685.
[4] Tracey, op. cit., p. 54.
[5] See below: Frederick County Land Records, WR 27-195, Trustees to Davis; WR 27-283, Davis to Trustees; and in particular JS 3-306, Davis to Warring.

compass" and was the second course, therefore, actually NE x E 20 perches? I feel very strongly that this was the case. Using that course produces a rectangle of five acres:

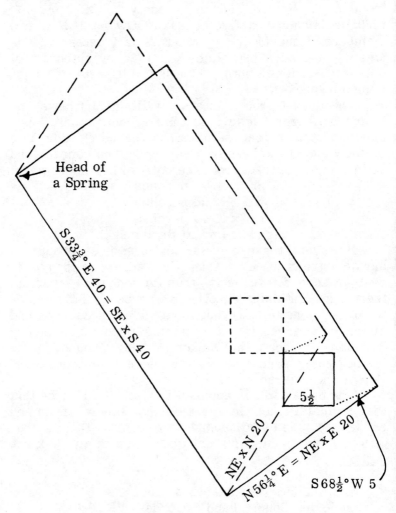

Head of a Spring

S33¾° E 40 = SE x S 40

NE x N 20

N56¼° E = NE x E 20

5½

S68½° W 5

FIVE-ACRE QUAKER TRACT
Scale: 1" = 10 perches
Broken Lines: as copied in Land Records
Solid Lines: to enclose a five-acre tract

In his deed Davis granted "full power and authority" to the trustees "to build thereon one or more house or houses for a Meeting Place for....the People called Quakers." This quotation and the courses and distances are from Frederick County Land Records WR 10-685 and WR 27-195 and from Prince George's County Land Records Y-21, 22, the original record of the deed.

Davis's "full power and authority" of 1739 may have been ex post facto, for Dr. Grace Tracey has told me that when Quaker Allen Farquhar died in 1738 he requested that he be buried at the "new Meeting House." Since there is no other meeting house known at that time in the surrounding area, it seems obvious that the reference is to the Monocacy Meeting House.

On June 29, 1751 Meredith Davis and his wife Ann sold 160 acres of GOOD LUCK to John Darnall for 124 pounds.[6] In this deed Davis states that he is conveying all that part of GOOD LUCK "on the west side of the Great Road that leads from the Mouth of Monocacy to Frederick Town, and is butted and bounded as follows: Begin at the end of the second line of the Resurvey of the said land and running thence

1. N 8° E 225
2. S 50½° E 146
3. S 21½° W   89
4. S 14° W   45
5. S 6° W   30
6. S 18½° W   59
7. Straight line to beginning"

Withheld from this 160-acre tract, however, are the five acres "where the Quaker Meeting House now stands and already conveyed by the said Meredith Davis for the use of the said Meeting."

The history of the Monocacy Meeting, sometimes called "The Cold Spring Meeting Of Monoquesey," is sketchy. There is evidence that in 1759 the meeting

---

[6] Frederick County Land Records, B-418.

house burned and that shortly thereafter another was built on the site. For reasons unknown, the membership apparently would not use the new building, and "on the 28th day of the 4th month, 1760" the Monocacy Meeting was abandoned.[7]

On February 9, 1792 Daniel Ballenger of Frederick County and William Matthews of York County, Pennsylvania, claiming that since the death of William Matthews and Henry Ballenger [original 1739 grantees] "the whole of said bargained premises has devolved on them," deed the five acres to eight trustees as joint tenants and not tenants in common, "to be held.....for the special purposes mentioned in the [original 1739] deed." The trustees were Anthony Poultney, Moses Farquhar, Joseph Hains, William Wood, Isaac Wright, William Ballenger, Amos Farquhar, and Stephen Howell.[8]

And then, on April 20, 1805, the above trustees — minus Stephen Howell, who had apparently died before that date — sold the five acres to Ignatius Davis for £47/10sh. Included therein was a "quarter acre" described as the Friends Burying Ground, which Davis agreed to deed back to the Quakers. The five acres are described as being that part of GOOD LUCK originally conveyed by Meredith Davis to William Matthews and Henry Ballenger [as trustees] on April 27, 1739.[9]

The grantors indicate that they are substitute trustees and refer to Land Record WR 10-685 for the source of their somewhat clouded title. They state that they are acting on instructions of "a meeting for sufferings held in Baltimore May 5, 1804," and recite that "William Wood, on behalf of the committee who had the care of the Meeting Land at Monoquesy," reported from inspection of the land the fixing of a price

---

[7] Tracey, op. cit., p. 62.
[8] Frederick County Land Records, WR 10-685.
[9] Ibid., WR 27-195.

10

of $40 per acre, but that the potential buyer, Ignatius Davis, grandson of Meredith Davis, the original owner of GOOD LUCK, would pay only $26.67 per acre unless the Friends would obtain an act of the Legislature confirming his title to it. They therefore decided to accept $26.67 and convey whatever title they had.

The 1805 deed recites that William Matthews died leaving Henry Ballenger as "sole surviving grantee" [in the 1739 deed], that Henry Ballenger died "sometime in 1774" leaving his son William Ballenger as "his heir at law," and that William Ballenger died "sometime" in 1787 "leaving his son Daniel Ballenger [as] his heir at law." The deed calls William Matthews [of the 1792 deed] heir at law of William Matthews, the original grantee. Apparently there was some doubt that the grantees in the 1792 deed were the sole survivors of the original 1739 grantees, and hence the cloud on the title they conveyed in April of 1805.[10]

On June 29, 1805 Ignatius Davis made good — in part — his agreement to deed back the Friends Burying Ground. His payment for the five acres at a price of $26.67 per acre was for only $4\frac{3}{4}$ acres, and he now deeds back not a quarter of an acre, but $30\frac{1}{4}$ [square] perches "by estimation." He charges £1/17/0 [$4.93] for that land.[11]

His deed was to Asa Moore of Lowden [sic] County, Virginia, William Stabler [Stapler] of Montgomery County, Maryland, and William Wood of Frederick County, Maryland, to be held in trust by the grantees "for the Religious Society of People called Quakers....with power to continue as a burial ground.... with leave to pass to and from the same, repair and keep up forever the enclosures thereof...." Davis describes the land conveyed as "being part of a tract... called GOOD LUCK."

---

[10] Ibid.
[11] Ibid., WR 27-283. $30\frac{1}{4}$ perches = 0.189 acre.

In the Davis deed of June 1805 the Friends Burying Ground is described as follows: Beginning at the end of 5 perches on a line drawn S 68½° W from the end of the second line of the five-acre tract, thence

N 5½
W 5½
S 5½

Straight line to beginning
30¼ [sq.] perches[12]

The 160-acre tract (Davis to Darnall in 1751), containing the five-acre Quaker tract, had passed by the will of John Darnall to his son John Darnall, Jr. In that will Darnall Senior devised to Darnall Junior lands described as "my dwelling plantation, being part of a tract....called CARROLLTON and a tract....called GOOD LUCK....a tract called MATTHEW'S LOTT.... and....one....called CONTENT."[13]

John Darnall, Jr., by his will probated January 19, 1797, devised most of his land to his brother Henry.[14]

Meanwhile, Ignatius Davis had acquired land near but not adjoining the five-acre Quaker tract and had had a resurvey made in 1798 which he called MOUNT HOPE, containing 566 acres.[15] The MOUNT HOPE mansion house was situated near and east of the Great Road to Fredericktown beyond the northern limits of present-day Buckeystown and hence was at least a mile from the Quaker Spring.

There is no evidence indicating when Davis began using water from the Spring, but he obviously had at least an oral right-of-way thereto through the Darnall land from Henry Darnall some time after 1797, and such a right-of-way may have existed prior to Henry Darnall's ownership.

---

[12] See sketch above, p. 8.
[13] Frederick County Will Records, A 1-309; probated February 9, 1768.
[14] Ibid., GM 3-154.
[15] Frederick County Survey Records, THO 1-152.

In 1801 Davis found — or said he found — an error in the original survey of the Darnall tract and sought to have it corrected. The resurvey showed $159\frac{1}{2}$ acres, less, of course, the five-acre Quaker Lot, which he did not acquire, as noted above, until 1805. Davis and Darnall confirmed the boundaries resulting from Davis's 1801 Resurvey by reciprocal deeds.[16]

This resurvey is valuable in orienting the Darnall tract surrounding the Quaker Spring property and identifying it as part of the original 1731 GOOD LUCK survey, for it places its first, or N $46\frac{1}{2}°$ W, line on the 17th line of CARROLLTON.

Henry Darnall, by his will probated November 13, 1809, devised all his property, real and personal, to his friend Henry Warring of Montgomery County. Darnall died in the District of Columbia and requested burial in the family burying ground "at my present dwelling" — which apparently referred to the old Darnall home near the Quaker Spring.[17]

If so, that would indicate a Darnall family cemetery, now obliterated. William J. Grove says of the Darnall mansion house that the house still stands at Rocky Fountain. He says also that some sixty years previously (c. 1868) when he visited the Darnall property the "family burying ground was surrounded by a brick wall."[18] Unfortunately, this family cemetery has suffered the fate of so many others, and there is no trace of it today.

In 1816 Davis and Warring executed reciprocal deeds whereby they exchanged certain tracts. The part of the transaction of interest here is its reference to the Quaker Spring. Davis conveyed to Warring $4\frac{3}{4}$ acres and $9\frac{3}{4}$ perches "known as the Quaker Lot," which he had bought from the Quaker trustees in 1805,

---

[16] Frederick County Land Records, WR 21-467, 545.
[17] Frederick County Will Records, RB 1-411.
[18] William J. Grove, History of Carrollton Manor, Frederick County, Maryland (Frederick, 1928), p. 24.

"excepting the Spring or United Springs of water thereon."[19]

Warring also granted Davis perpetual right-of-way through his lands "from where the said Ignatius Davis's house now stands to the Spring....now in use upon the land called the Quaker Lot....at all times to and from said Spring....in the same....manner as he used the.... path or footway during the lifetime of Henry Darnall."

On August 10, 1844 Henry Warring's widow, Milicent Warring, sold to Davis Richardson, for a consideration of $18,423.75, the lands which are described as "now called ROCKY FOUNTAIN....composed, in part, of CARROLLTON....GOOD LUCK.... and MOUNT HOPE." Mention is made of the $159\frac{1}{2}$ acres of the 1801 resurvey, "including a lot of 5 acres belonging to the Society of Friends." The deed states that the second line of this $159\frac{1}{2}$-acre tract is in the 16th line of CARROLLTON. It reaffirms the perpetual "right of use of a Spring on said land, known as the Quaker Spring, according to the terms of [Ignatius Davis's] contract with Henry Warring."[20]

It also excepts "the land occupied for two graveyards, known respectively as the Family and Quaker graveyards....together with ingress and egress at all times." The term "family graveyard" obviously refers to the Darnall family cemetery, since the major part of the Warring lands had been inherited from Henry Darnall.

If the 160-acre tract (Davis to Darnall, 1751) or that tract resurveyed for $159\frac{1}{2}$ acres (1801) can be definitely fitted into the original (1731) GOOD LUCK survey and its relation to adjoining lands established, then the location of the Quaker Lot and Burying Ground should no longer be in doubt. Fortunately, this is not too difficult.

In 1799 the boundaries of Charles Carroll's

---

[19] Frederick County Land Records, JS3-306/307.
[20] Ibid., HS22-409ff.

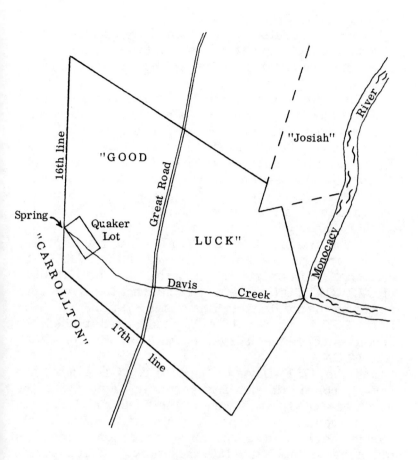

GOOD LUCK

Scale: 1" = 100 perches

Based on a comparison of Map #3 in Tracey, op. cit.,
and a 1799 Plat of CARROLLTON included in Frederick
County Land Record WR 19-535ff. Superimposed are
the courses and distances of Meredith Davis's transfer
in 1751 of 160 acres to John Darnall (Ibid., B-418).
The latter define the "Great Road that leads from the
Mouth of Monocacy to Frederick Town" (cf. text
above, p. 9). The Great Road is now known as Maryland Route #85.

15

10,000-acre CARROLLTON were resurveyed by a commission. From that survey a large-scale and apparently very accurate plat was made and filed with the report.[21]

This plat indicates the location of some adjoining surveys and bears some very accurately located landmarks. The Frederick Road appears carefully laid on, as does the Davis Creek, now known as Rocky Fountain Run, which flows through present-day Buckeystown. Also shown, at the 16th line, is a spring from which that Creek begins. The spring is unnamed, but in view of all previous findings, it can only be the Quaker Spring.

If the original 1731 GOOD LUCK survey is platted to the same scale and superimposed on the CARROLLTON plat, it fits perfectly along the 16th and 17th lines of CARROLLTON. One may recall that the Davis 1801 resurvey placed its first line on the 17th line of CARROLLTON, and the 1844 Warring deed placed the second line of that survey on the 16th line of CARROLLTON.

If the 1751 (Davis to Darnall) deed is platted and superimposed, it also fits perfectly, embodying the whole of GOOD LUCK west of the Frederick Road. Its eastern contours follow those platted for the road, although the 1751 deed doesn't so state. In spite of its slight variations, the 1801 resurvey, superimposed, fits almost as accurately.

Finally, if the five-acre Quaker Lot is platted to the same scale and laid on, with its beginning point at the spring shown on the CARROLLTON plat, its relation to the whole is seen — though not its exact location, since this can be determined only by survey.

Since 1844, the Warring property has been fragmented among a number of owners, but at least 140 acres, still known as ROCKY FOUNTAIN FARM, is owned by Franz S. and Myrtle A. Blue.[22] The Blue

---

[21] Ibid., WR 19-535ff.

house stands perhaps fifty yards southwest of the site of the Darnall mansion house, of which the large brick chimney alone remains. The water for the Blue household is drawn by pipeline from the Quaker Spring.

The Blue house is about four-tenths of a mile west of Buckeystown and is reached by a road leading westward from the present Maryland Route #85 about midway between the northern edge of town and Maryland Route #80. This road, incidentally, is quite probably part of that petitioned for in 1745 to the Prince George's Court to be laid out "from the Main Road above Isaac Leonard's [Fullmer's Station] along by Baltis Fout's so as to come into the Main Minoccocee Road by [way of] the Quaker Meeting House."[23] If so, it was one of the oldest public roads in Frederick County. However, by Equity Suit No. 17456, decided in 1953, the Blues had it declared a private roadway.

I have been primarily concerned here with the land history of the Quaker Meeting House and its location in present-day terms. For a more detailed history of the Monocacy Meeting and the families comprising it, see the Hopewell Friends History[24] and works by Dr. Tracey,[25] W. W. Hinshaw[26] and T. C. Matlack.[27]

---

[22] Ibid., 452-80, January 21, 1946.

[23] Tracey, op. cit., Map #7 and p. 61.

[24] Hopewell Friends History, 1734-1934, Frederick County, Virginia (Strasburg, Virginia, 1936), pp. 54-55, 70, 217, 220, 542-543.

[25] Tracey, op. cit.

[26] William Wade Hinshaw, Encyclopedia of American Quaker Genealogy (Ann Arbor, Michigan, 1950), vol. 6, pp. 357 et seq., 463 et seq.

[27] T. Chalkley Matlack, "Historical Sketches of Friends' Meetings" (typescript, Moorestown, N. J., 1938). Copy at Friends Historical Library, Swarthmore College, Pennsylvania.

SOME HISTORICAL NOTES ON JEFFERSON, MD.

Incorporated in 1832 from the Towns Of
NEW TOWN (TRAP) and NEW FREEDOM

    This is not a history of the Town of Jefferson. It is what the above title implies, with particular emphasis on the early land history of the two towns from which Jefferson was formed. I shall also try to correct several erroneous statements which, over the years, have appeared in print — notably, for instance, that New Town was laid out by Bernard Hershperger.

    Apparently there were no houses built in what is now Jefferson before 1774, for in that year a town was laid out there and called New Town. I find nothing in the records to indicate that any buildings were standing on the lots at the time they were laid off.

    So far as I am able to learn, this was the third planned town in what is now Frederick County, preceded only by Frederick city and Middletown.[1] In this connection, and primarily in order to record material I have from time to time found in the Land Records, it may be of interest to list the dates of beginning of certain towns, including two which are now in Washington County and one in Carroll County.

---

[1] See below, pp. 137-148. There is no recorded early plat of Middletown, but beginning on March 3, 1767 George Michael Jesserong began selling numbered lots there, subject to ground rents payable to himself and his heirs. It seems apparent, therefore, that he laid out the town early in 1767. The first such sale is recorded in Frederick County Land Records, K-956.

The following shows the date of the first lot sale in the several towns, by whom sold, and the Frederick County Land Record reference to each:

1762	Taneytown	Raphael Taney	H-157
1764	Sharpsburg	Joseph Chapline	J-109
1767	Middletown	Geo. Michael Jesserong	K-956
1768	Funkstown (Jerusalemtown)	Jacob Funk	L-583
1774	Jefferson (New Town)	Leonard Smith for Mrs. Eleanor Medley	See below, p. 24
1779	Creagerstown	John Creager	WR 2-360
1782	Libertytown	John Young	WR 6-381
1785	Emmitsburg	Samuel Emmit	WR 6- 82
1786	Woodsboro (Woodsberry Town)	Joseph Wood	WR 6-313
1787	Brunswick (Berlin)	Leonard Smith	WR 7-525
1793	New Market	Nicholas Hale	WR 11-591
1815	Lewistown	Daniel Fundenburg	JS 1-363
1784	Point of Rocks (Trammelstown)		Will GM 2-53[2]

Dr. Grace L. Tracey of Hampstead, Maryland, who had done extensive research into the early land history of Frederick County, told me that in some early records she came across a reference to one Flayl Payne, who was named by the Prince George's County Court in 1738 as a road supervisor for the road running from the general vicinity of Jefferson to the mouth of the Monocacy River. This indicates that there was traffic — and undoubtedly, therefore, settlers — through the section years before New Town was platted.

----

[2] This reference is to the will of John Trammel who directed his executors to lay out a town of 400 lots. I have found no record of lot sales. Scharf in his <u>History of Western Maryland</u> states that the town was located a mile from present-day Point of Rocks and burned down. I have made no effort to verify this.

Moreover, I think it is rather obvious that New Town was laid out on a road already established, perhaps from Frederick to Harper's Ferry or to Crampton's Gap, because otherwise the town would certainly have been platted with the street parallel to the northern boundary of the tract on which it was located. Instead, the northern boundary runs N 85° E, whereas the street runs approximately N 80° E.

New Town was laid out by Leonard Smith for Mrs. Eleanor Medley, a widow. She may have come originally from St. Mary's County, although Medley Election District in Montgomery County, then part of Frederick County, is probably named for her husband's family, and she may also have been from that section.

By a deed dated November 15, 1774, Mrs. Medley purchased from Melcor Tabler 98 acres of a tract called LOW LAND, which began "near the head of a branch of Kittocton Creek called Prick Run...." and 3 acres of CHILDREN'S CHANCE.[3] The farm situated just south of, and adjoining Jefferson, until recently owned by Herschel Boyer, is comprised principally of the remnants of the Medley land.

Tabler had purchased this land on August 22, 1764 from Thomas Ray,[4] and in a survey record under date of December 21, 1801[5] we find reference to this land's having been granted on June 20, 1740 to Daniel Johnson Low for 100 acres — hence the name LOW LAND.[6]

New Town was laid out on LOW LAND. Unfortunately, Smith never took the trouble to file his plat of

---

[3] Frederick County Land Records, BD 1-165.

[4] Ibid., J-723.

[5] Frederick County Survey Records, THO 2-299/300.

[6] In Frederick County Land Records, BD 2-189, there is recorded under date of November 13, 1775 a deed from Leonard Smith, Bennett Neale and Elizabeth Sprigg Neale, his wife, to Bernard Hershperger, which traces the chain of title of LOW LAND from Low to Medley.

20

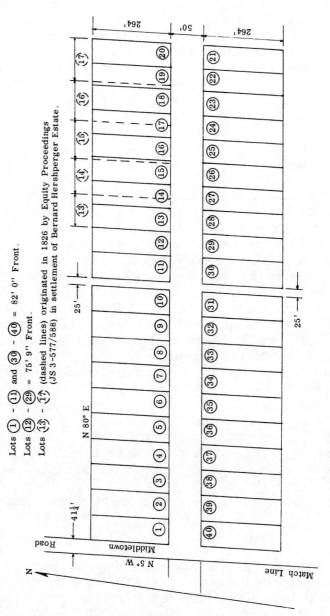

Lots ① - ⑪ and ㉚ - ㊵ = 82' 0" Front.

Lots ⑫ - ㉙ = 75' 9" Front.

Lots ⑬ - ⑰ (dashed lines) originated in 1826 by Equity Proceedings (JS 3-577/588) in settlement of Bernard Hershperger Estate.

PLAT OF "NEW TOWN" AS LAID OUT IN 1774
BY LEONARD SMITH FOR MRS. ELEANOR MEDLEY
(Reconstruction by Millard M. Rice, 1960)

21

New Town, but I am able to state with certainty that Lot No. 1 was at the northeast corner of present Main Street in Jefferson and the road leading to Middletown. The present (1975) owner of this lot, now known as Lot No. 12 on the Plat of Jefferson, is R. E. Houck.

There were in all 40 lots laid out — 20 on each side of Main Street.[7] Beginning at No. 1, the numbers ran eastward along the north side of the street to a point opposite the western edge of the present Lander Road.[8] Lot No. 21 was then located on the south side of Main Street adjoining Lander Road on the west. It is now known as Lot No. 31 on the Plat of Jefferson. Numbering of the lots continued westward from No. 21 along the south side of Main Street to a point opposite the eastern edge of the old Middletown Road, and this was the western boundary of Lot No. 40.

Thus an extension southward across Main Street of the line forming the east side of the Middletown Road was the western boundary of New Town. But this was not the western boundary of LOW LAND. That was the western edge of the old Middletown Road, which would indicate that some time between 1740 when LOW LAND was granted to Daniel Low and 1774 when New Town was laid out, the road to Middletown was cut through on the western edge of LOW LAND.

By reference to a survey of Lot No. 40 in New Town,[9] it is shown that this lot was conveyed on June 30, 1787 by John Smith, son of Leonard Smith, to Henry Filling. In the deed from Smith to Filling the width of the main street of New Town is stated to be 50 feet.[10]

The lots in New Town were sold for £5 each and

---

[7] See p. 21.

[8] This road was long known as the Potomac Road or the Road to Luckett's Ferry, and I think it is unfortunate that it is no longer known as the Potomac Road.

[9] Frederick County Survey Records, THO 1-163.

[10] Frederick County Land Records, WR 7-371.

22

Ground rents due on Lots in New Town, since called Jefferson
In Frederick County up to 30th Aug. 1832.
at 6 pence per Lott Annually

Boteler	on	Lots Nos. 1 & 2	$2.93	pd. in part $1.00
Church	"	half Lot No. 3	.33⅓	pd. in full
Church	"	half Lot No. 3 & part lot	.91	pd. in part .81
		No. 4 containing 52 feet	.91	
Blessing	"	parts of No. 4 & No. 5 - 71 feet	1.26	
Mr. Larned	"	part of No. 5 - 72	.58	
Torrance	"	Lot No. 6	1.36	
Little	"	¼ of No. 7	.26	
McGill	"	¾ of No. 7 & No. 8	1.85	pd. in full
Torrance	"	Lot No. 9	1.06	
D. Keller	"	Lot No. 10	1.46	pd. 1.60
Culler	"	Lot No. 11	1.06	
Culler	"	Lot No. 12	1.06	
Mrs. Wiles	"	Lot No. 30	3.32	
Burckheardt	"	Lot No. 31	.66	pd. in part .40
Dare	"	Lot No. 32	1.06	
Hoffman	"	Lot No. 33	1.06	
_. Kesler	"	Lot No. 34 & part of 35	1.61	
Johnson	"	Lot part of 35 fifty two feet	.66	pd. in part .52
Dorsey	"	Lots Nos. 37 & 38	6.52⅔	pd. in part 5.20
Mrs. Kesler	"	Lot No. 36	1.06	
C. Tabler	"	Lot No. 39	1.06	
Mrs. Murry	"	Lot No. 40 - one half	1.53⅔	pd. in part .20
Garray	"	Lot No. 40 - the other half	1.53⅔	

Nos. 13, 14, 15, 16, 17, 18, 19 & 20, 21, 22, 23, 24, 25, 26, 27, 28 & 29
It does not appear that these lots were deeded by the Executor of Eleanor
Medley, but were held by Bernard Hersperger, the owner of the tract of
Land out of which the Town was laid off and at his death claimed by his
heirs, except those that he had conveyed in his life, nor is it known that
they are subject to ground rents.

Note by MMR: The notation just above is apparently in error. By terms of
purchase, Hersperger was obligated to pay ground rent on lots he bought,
which were Nos. "11 to 16 inclusive and 18 to 29 inclusive." (Frdk. Co.
Land Records, BD 2-189.) With 6 pence = 6⅔ cents, rents on Lots Nos.
30, 37 and 38 had not been paid for 50 years, and no rents had been paid on
any lots for at least 10 years.

(This schedule was obtained from a friend. Its source is unknown.)

were subject to a ground rent of 6 pence per year, payable to Mrs. Medley's heirs, as directed in her will.[11] In an article on Jefferson, published in the semi-weekly edition of the Frederick "News" of September 5, 1922, it is stated that ground rents were paid on Jefferson lots until 1824. I do not know the authority for this statement but can demonstrate from the tabulation on the preceding page that, although ground rents were paid on one or two lots as late as 1822, most lots were in arrears from about 1815 and no ground rent had been paid on some since about 1788.

Mrs. Medley died late in 1774, for her will is dated December 22, 1774 and was probated January 5, 1775.[12] In it she appointed Leonard Smith as her executor and directed that LOW LAND and CHILDREN'S CHANCE be sold, "all but what is laid off for a town." Endorsed on the back of the will is a direction to her executor to "give deeds for all the lots in New Town which I have not given deeds for." Obviously, therefore, some lots were sold in New Town in 1774, but I find no evidence of any deeds signed by Mrs. Medley.

The following is a list of the first 22 lots sold in New Town. All deeds were made by Leonard Smith, executor of Eleanor Medley, and nearly all were dated January 16, 1775. All lots were either described as having an 82-foot frontage, or that dimension can be calculated from adjoining lot descriptions. Their depth was 264 feet. Except as noted, courses are given as N 85° E and S 5° E. Listed here in order are lot numbers, Land Record references, grantees, and, where shown, grantees' occupations:

1   WR 1-376   Charles Neale (son of Bennett Neale, deceased, of St. Mary's County)
2   BD 1-130   Abraham Leakins, farmer

---

[11] Recorded twice: Frdk. Co. Wills A 1-527, GM 1-47.
[12] Ibid. The date was just five weeks after her purchase of LOW LAND.

3	BD 1- 94	Francis Hoofman, farmer
4	BD 1-138	Joseph Leakins, farmer
5	BD 1-135	Michael Walker, farmer
6	BD 1-140	Michael Tabler, farmer
7	BD 1-126	Andrew Kessler, shoemaker
8	BD 1-122	Heronemous Hildebrand, farmer
0	WR 27-379	Bennett Heard, farmer
10	BD 1-281	Thomas Taylor, farmer
17	BD 1-133	Bennett Heard, farmer
30	BD 1-331	Conrad Reeker, blacksmith
31	BD 1-118	John Smith of L., wheelwright
32	BD 1-375	Francis Smith, son of Leonard
33	BD 1- 94	Francis Hoofman, farmer
34	BD 1-120	Gabriel Thomas, farmer
35	BD 1-140	Melcor Tabler, farmer
36	BD 1-128	Felty Thomas, farmer (for some reason the courses of this lot are given as N 82° E, N 5° W)
37	BD 1-109	George Ransburgh, farmer
38	BD 1-109	George Ransburgh, farmer
39	BD 1-130	Abraham Leakins, farmer
40	BD 1-118	John Smith of L., wheelwright

With the exception of Lot Nos. 17 and 30, all these lots lay west of the center alleys, indicating that the early life of the town centered in the western half.

To a considerable extent, the story of the early settlement of Western Maryland is that of Englishmen first acquiring land by grant or purchase and then re-selling it to the later settlers, mostly Germans, who were coming into the territory. This is strikingly the case in New Town. Mrs. Medley, Leonard Smith, and the Neales were obviously English. Obedient to terms of Mrs. Medley's will, Smith and the Neales, by the deed referred to above[13] on November 13, 1775 sold LOW LAND, CHILDREN'S CHANCE and 18 lots

---

[13] Frederick County Land Records, BD 2-189. See above, p. 20, note 6.

in New Town to Bernard Hershperger, a German.

The deed is most interesting. It conveys to Hershperger 98 acres of LOW LAND and 3 acres of CHILDREN'S CHANCE "(except 22....lots....in....New Town situate on part of said land, to wit: Nos. 1 to 10, inclusive, No. 17, and Nos. 30 to 40 inclusive)." It recites further with respect to Hershperger that he is "yielding and paying for 18 lots yearly and every year on the first day of November....6 pence current money for each of the lots, to wit: Nos. 11 to 16 inclusive and Nos. 18 to 29 inclusive, unto Elizabeth Sprigg Neale, wife of Bennett Neale and after her demise....unto ye children of Elizabeth Sprigg Neale to be equally divided among her heirs." This was ground rent. The purchase price of the whole tract was £195 current money of the Province of Maryland.

I have been able to reconstruct, with what I believe is reasonable accuracy, a plat of New Town a copy of which is shown on page 21. The lots referred to above, therefore, were as follows on the present plat of the Town of Jefferson: Nos. 11 to 16, inclusive, in New Town are Nos. 24, 25, 26, 27 and the western part of 28 in Jefferson. Nos. 18 to 20, inclusive, are Nos. 30 and the major eastern portion of No. 29 in Jefferson. Nos. 21 to 29, inclusive, are Nos. 31 to 39, inclusive, on the present plat of Jefferson.

Perhaps I should preface all of what follows by saying that early land surveying — and some not so early, for that matter — being what it was, and is, I have found it impossible to reconcile many courses and distances in connection with New Town and Jefferson. For that reason I am sure my reconstruction is only approximately correct.

I have previously stated that the western edge of the Middletown Road was the western boundary of LOW LAND. There are numerous proofs of this in the land records, but perhaps the most obvious is RESURVEY ON THE TITLE IS GOOD, made for Bernard Hershperger in 1798. This resurvey embraced LOW LAND, part of the RESURVEY ON WELLS INVENTION and part of CHILDREN'S CHANCE.[14]

In this resurvey it is shown that the 17th line of THE TITLE IS GOOD, which is also the northern boundary of New Town as originally laid out, is $97\frac{1}{2}$ perches in length, measured from the eastern, or fourth, line of LOW LAND. That leaves $2\frac{1}{2}$ perches, or $41\frac{1}{4}$ feet, from the western edge of New Town to the western, or second, line of LOW LAND. Hence $41\frac{1}{4}$ feet was allowed for the Middletown Road.[15]

On the basis of this calculation, therefore, Smith had $1,608\frac{3}{4}$ feet to divide into 20 lots. He made all the lots from Nos. 1 to 10 inclusive (north side of the street) and Nos. 31 to 40 inclusive (south side of the street) with frontages of 82 feet. All of the original (1775) deeds for these lots recite this width.

This brought him eastward as far as the alleys in the center of the town. These he laid out as 25 feet wide.[16] The alley leading south from the street is referred to in the deed of Smith, acting as executor of Medley, which was dated January 6, 1775 and which conveyed Lot No. 31 to his son John Smith of L. The alley is described as being 25 feet wide "for the use of ye town."[17]

Likewise, the deed of Smith, Executor, to Conrad Reeker, blacksmith, for Lot No. 30 on the east side of this alley refers to the 25-foot alley.[18] It also lists the frontage of No. 30 as 82 feet.

Now, deducting $41\frac{1}{4}$ feet, 820 feet (for 10 lots of 82 feet frontage) and 25 feet for the alley from 1650 feet, the width of LOW LAND, left Smith $763\frac{3}{4}$ feet for

---

[14] Frederick County Survey Records, THO 1-163.

[15] Johnson shows this as $41\frac{1}{2}$ feet on his 1832 plat of Jefferson. See pp. 38-39.

[16] Johnson, ibid., shows the alley on the north side of the street as 13 feet.

[17] Frederick County Land Records, BD 1-118.

[18] Ibid., BD 1-221.

his 10 lots east of the alley on the south side of the street. But we know that one of the lots, No. 30, east of the alley was 82 feet wide. Hence he then had $681\frac{3}{4}$ feet for the remaining nine lots, which, evenly divided, would give each of the nine a frontage of $75\frac{3}{4}$ feet.

For all the errors Smith made in his survey, I'm quite sure he was no ignoramus. Obviously, therefore, the thing to do was to give the remaining nine lots $75\frac{3}{4}$ feet frontage and his plat would be complete. I strongly suspect that is what he did, and I have reconstructed his plat on that assumption.

This assumption is borne out in part at least by a deed recorded on June 9, 1828.[19] This is a deed from George Ramsburg, Trustee of Henry Hershperger (who had become incompetent), to Sebastian Ramsburg, conveying Lot Nos. 21 and 22, wherein reference is made to "each of said lots containing 74 feet, 8 inches front on the Main Street...." The slight difference ($75\frac{3}{4}$ feet versus 74 feet, 8 inches) may be explained by the fact that none of the lots from No. 21 to No. 29, inclusive, was sold or transferred until more than 20 years after 1775, and doubtless in that time whatever landmarks Smith erected in identifying lot boundaries had been pretty well obliterated.

Two facts point to the possibility that there may have been one or more log houses built on some of these lots. One of these, and the most obvious, is the existence of the old log back parts of houses now standing on some of these lots — notably on Nos. 21 and 22 (Nos. 31 and 32 in Jefferson). The log parts of the houses now on those two lots would seem by their very age and type of construction to antedate 1828.

The other fact is the sale by Bernard Hershperger on January 18, 1798 of Lot No. 28 to Jacob Karn for £36 — a price which seems to indicate purchase of something more than a vacant lot which 23 years pre-

---

[19]   Ibid., JS 29-589.

viously had sold for £5.[20]

On June 26, 1798 Bernard Hershperger transferred, for a nominal consideration, Lot Nos. 23, 24,
25, 26 and 27 to his five daughters and No. 29 to his
son Henry.[21] The five lots went respectively to Eve,
Mary (May), Elizabeth (Young), Dorothy (Kemp), and
Barbary (Kemp). No. 24 would be approximately No.
34 in Jefferson, and on it is one of the log back rooms
previously mentioned. Likewise, on No. 27 (approximately No. 37 in Jefferson) log construction also
exists. These log buildings could have been — and
probably were — built by the Hershperger daughters
and their husbands, for 1798 was still a time of log
construction.

It seems to me quite possible that the Hershperger
daughters and their successor owners, possibly oblit-
erating the original lot markers, may not have been
too careful of their boundary lines. Hence, fences as
erected probably followed more or less arbitrary property boundaries, rather than the exact courses and
distances originally platted by Smith. All of this may
well account for the variation in lot frontages as they
apparently existed when Jefferson was platted in 1832.

Before I discuss the north side of the street east
of the central alley, I should point out that the deeds
for all the lots sold before Bernard Hershperger bought
the remainder — and many of the later deeds as well —
are described as having courses running N 85° E and
S 5° E. It is interesting to speculate why Smith thought
he was running a course of N 85° E, which would have
been parallel to the northern boundary of LOW LAND.

He was, I am convinced, laying out his town on an
existing road which, when the town was replatted in
1832, was said to run N 80° E.[22] The courses given

---

[20]   Ibid., WR 16-159.
[21]   Ibid., WR 17-109/116.
[22]   Without running that course today on a true azi-
muth, it would be difficult to say what its true course

for the front lines of these lots varied, but all boundaries between lots were always given as S 5° E.

The alley running northward from Main Street is shown on the plat of Jefferson as being 13 feet wide. It was, however, definitely laid out as 25 feet wide, for Smith's deed to Thomas Taylor of March 28, 1775 for Lot No. 10 refers to it as adjoining a 25-foot alley "for the public use of said Town."[23] I think there is no doubt that at some time one or both adjoining lots encroached on the alley.

Actually, I strongly suspect, the major encroachment was by the property east of the alley, as the following rather definitely seems to indicate. On August 8, 1792 Bernard Hershperger transferred Lot Nos. 11 and 12 to his son Henry.[24] There is an old log backbuilding on No. 11, flush with the present eastern edge of the alley, which was doubtless built by Henry shortly after he acquired the lots. Perhaps he felt that since his father owned such a substantial part of the town, he could build just about wherever he pleased, regardless of platted boundaries.

Thirty-six years later, on August 1, 1828, George Ramsburg, as trustee of Henry Hershperger, deeded these two lots to Henry Culler, describing each as having 82-foot frontage.[25] Yet just four years later, on the 1832 plat of Jefferson, they are shown with $87\frac{1}{2}$-foot frontage. The difference is therefore 11 feet which, added to the 13 feet shown as the alley width, gives 24 feet, just one foot less than its original width.

But the greatest violence to Smith's original plat was done to the eight lots between the eastern boundary of Lot No. 12 and the eastern end of town. By his will,

---

actually is. Various deed references, surveys, resurveys and recorded agreements give variations from N 79° E to N 82° E.

[23] Frederick County Land Records, BD 1-281.
[24] Ibid., WR 11-3.
[25] Ibid., JS 30-4.

Bernard Hershperger left these eight lots to his five daughters or their heirs, to be divided equally between them.[26] The Frederick County Court, sitting in Equity on August 2, 1824, appointed Henry Culler, Patrick McGill, Sr., William Lynch, George Hoffman, and James Wiles as commissioners to make this division. On April 13, 1826 the Court received their report and ordered that it become effective in accordance with a plat prepared by the commissioners. Out of the original eight lots, this plat created five lots of irregular dimensions and accordingly made the last lot at the east end on the north side of the street No. 17 instead of No. 20 as platted by Smith.[27]

The dimensions of these five new and arbitrary lots as shown on the 1832 plat are not quite the same as those of the commissioners' 1826 plat, but they are so close thereto that they have been indicated on my reconstructed plat as they appeared in 1832 in order to avoid almost completely overlapping lines.

Moreover, on my plat I have shown the north side of the street the same as the south side, on the assumption that there is no good reason to believe that Smith laid it out otherwise. It would have been a little foolish, it seems to me, for him to create one lot of 82 feet width east of the alley on the south side of the street and two such lots on the north side. This is true if for no other reasons than the recalculation involved. I have said that in my opinion Smith was intelligent and, I suspect, in a hurry, for he was doubtlessly already planning in his mind the platting of Brunswick (Berlin), which he accomplished in 1787.

The success of New Town influenced Elias DeLashmutt, Jr., to lay out another town adjoining New Town on the west, which was called New Freedom. I cannot say definitely when this was actually done, but I have found a deed from DeLashmutt to George Willyard,

---

[26] Frederick County Will Records, GM3-242/245.
[27] Frederick County Equity Records, JS3-577/588.

31

dated January 17, 1795, for Lot No. 6 "in the addition to New Town, called New Freedom," the lot having 60 feet frontage and "adjoining the alley leading to the spring."[28]

This is apparently the first sale of a lot in New Freedom. Like Smith, DeLashmutt never troubled to file his plat. But I have been able to reconstruct the original plat of New Freedom with what I believe is reasonable accuracy, and a copy is shown on page 33.

With respect to New Freedom, I can state rather definitely that Lot No. 1 was just across the Middletown Road from Lot No. 1 in New Town, because I find a deed dated February 21, 1826 from Philip Culler to Christian Sifford, conveying "Lot No. 2 in New Freedom....being one of a parcel of lots laid off by a certain Elias DeLashmutt near New Town, the same being 60 feet front and running back 182 feet and lying next to the corner lot on the road leading from New Town to Middletown...."[29]

At least 22 lots were originally laid out in New Freedom, each apparently 60 feet front and 182 feet deep, but so far I have been able to identify definitely only 17 of them. Apparently what is now Lot No. 1 in Jefferson was not Lot No. 11 in New Freedom (as it would normally appear), for No. 11 was what is now No. 55 in Jefferson. Lot No. 61 in Jefferson was therefore No. 17 in New Freedom.

While No. 61 is the last platted lot in Jefferson, a look at the plat (see pp. 38-39) will show that there was room for four more lots between No. 61 and the western boundary of the town. If these were originally platted, they would have been Nos. 18, 19, 20 and 21. Then No. 22 could have been, for reasons unknown, what is now No. 1 on the plat of Jefferson.

This assumption is borne out by a deed dated May 19, 1810 from Arthur Boteler to Christian Sifford,

---

[28] Frederick County Land Records, WR 13-39.
[29] Ibid., JS 24-319.

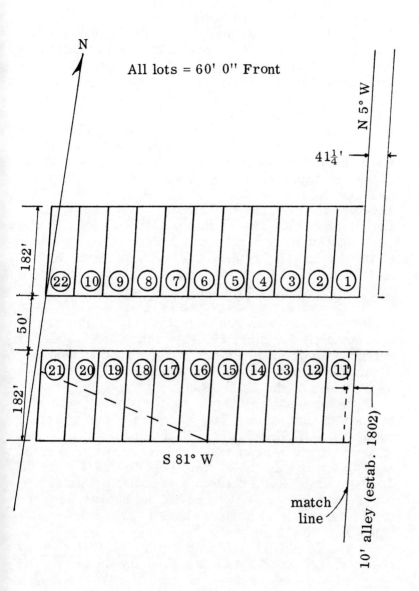

PLAT OF "NEW FREEDOM"
AS LAID OUT ABOUT 1795 BY ELIAS DELASHMUTT
(Reconstruction by Millard M. Rice, 1960)

wherein for $250 Boteler sold to Sifford "those five lots of land lying in a small town laid out by Elias De-Lashmutt.... called New Freedom, nearly adjoining New Town," being numbers 7, 8, 9, 10 and 22, "adjoining each other and lying on the north side and adjoining the main road....from Fredericktown to Harper's Ferry on the Potomack...."[30]

Sifford owned these five lots until 1843/45, but meanwhile, in 1832, New Freedom and New Town were merged into the one town of Jefferson and the whole was replatted (see again pp. 38-39). On the new plat, Lot Nos. 7, 8, 9 and 10 of New Freedom became Lot Nos. 5, 4, 3 and 2 of Jefferson. When on August 7, 1843 Sifford sold some of this property to John Ervin, he described it as comprising 10 feet on the west side of the Methodist Protestant Church property and 21 feet, 4 inches of land between the Church property and Lot No. 3, together with Lot Nos. 4 and 5.[31]

Quite obviously, therefore, the M. P. Church occupied some of this land before 1843. However, it was not until February 25, 1845 that a deed was recorded from Sifford to Peter Boyer, Thomas Johnson, Richard Chilcoat, Levin Rice and Perry G. Rice [Jr.] as Trustees of the M. P. Church.[32]

The property conveyed to the Church was described as commencing 10 feet from the line of a tract known as DANIEL'S DILLIGENCE and running $91\frac{1}{2}$ feet to John Ervin's property, which, according to the deed to Ervin was the western edge of Lot No. 3. If Lot No. 22 in New Freedom was actually what is now No. 1 in Jefferson, Sifford didn't so indicate in either of his deeds, so that somewhere in this exchange of titles Lot No. 22 got lost.

I should add a brief reference to the 10-foot alley shown at Lot No. 11 with a broken line in my recon-

---

[30] Ibid., WR 37-328.
[31] Ibid., HS 20-254.
[32] Ibid., WBT 2-221.

34

structed plat of New Freedom, and in solid line on Johnson's 1832 plat of Jefferson between Lot Nos. 54 and 55.

This alley was not a part of the original plan of New Freedom. But by deed dated June 26, 1802, Elias DeLashmutt sold acreage lying south of New Freedom to Patrick McGill.[33] DeLashmutt covenanted to lay off an alley 10 feet wide through the east side of Lot No. 11 in New Freedom, "said alley to begin at....the Main Road....for the express purpose of giving said McGill and his heirs a free and uninterrupted intercourse from said Main Road to the said land hereby conveyed, which alley shall always be kept open for the purposes aforesaid."

I have not traced the later history of this alley, but presume it is still dedicated for the use of the owners of the land purchased in 1802 by McGill from DeLashmutt.

New Freedom got its name from the tract of land on which it was laid out. The tract was actually made up of two parcels, including 88 acres on CHILDREN'S CHANCE granted DeLashmutt on November 8, 1764 and $4\frac{1}{2}$ acres on SHORT COMMONS granted him on July 1, 1793. The original grants which comprised New Freedom were found to be foul of other grants — a common experience — and a resurvey by DeLashmutt dated December 14, 1801 reduced the tract to 86 acres.[34]

Because of the fact that neither the plat for New Town nor that for New Freedom was filed in the land records of the County and because the early-day surveyors apparently did a rather poor job, causing the lots, particularly in New Town, not to run true with their stated courses and distances, certain of the influential residents of the two towns, whose names are not mentioned in any sources I have seen, decided that

---

[33] Ibid., WR 23-480. Recorded November 5, 1802.
[34] Frederick County Survey Records, THO 2-299.

the two towns should be combined into one, replatted and incorporated. Accordingly, by Chapter 299 of the Acts of the Maryland Legislature of 1831, there was passed on March 14, 1832 "an Act to blend New Town (Trap) and New Freedom....into one [town] by the name of Jefferson.

A commission composed of three men, whose names I decipher as William Lynch, Levy Williss and John W. Pratt, was appointed to resurvey and replat the new town. The plat of Jefferson, recorded on July 2, 1832,[35] is the result of their labors. It is a copy of the original plat prepared in June 1832 by Thomas Johnson, a son of William Johnson. See pages 38-39.

The lots of the two earlier towns were renumbered, Lot No. 1 being on the north side of Main Street at the west end of town, with the numbers extending eastward to No. 30. No. 31 was the first number on the south side of Main Street and was the same lot as No. 21 in the original plan of New Town. Numbers on the south side of the street ran westward to the western end of the town or, according to the courses endorsed on the new plat, to Lot No. 63.

However, the plat actually shows only 61 lots, a fact which is unexplained and which seems to indicate that the new surveyors may not have been any more careful in their work than their predecessors. My own candid opinion, after study of early land grants, resurveys and the 1832 plat of Jefferson, is that there is still considerable doubt as to the complete accuracy of that plat.

Endorsed on the new Jefferson plat is the following: "The original depth of lots were [sic] 264 feet.[36] Commissioners have thought proper to add $8\frac{1}{2}$ feet, the width of sidewalks, making the depth of lots that much

---

[35] Frederick County Land Records, JS 39-257.
[36] This applied only to New Town, but it is not so stated.

more. The breadth of street laid down at 51 feet including sidewalks."

The 1831 Act of the Legislature declared that the seat of government should be in a "house occupied as a tavern by Daniel Shower" [Shawen, Showen] and that "the limits of the said Jefferson shall extend to the distance of one-fourth mile from the tavern aforesaid, each way." By scale measurement of the 1832 Plat, it appears that this tavern might have been located on Lot No. 19 or Lot No. 44 of Jefferson.

Lot No. 19, on the north side of Main Street, contains a small house now owned by Gerald J. Pendley. But I can find no evidence that this property was ever used as a tavern. Lot No. 44, on the south side of Main Street is now the site of the United Church of Christ (Reformed) parsonage. The large dwelling replaced by the parsonage in 1967 was one of the older houses in Jefferson, and its east wing had at various times been occupied by a store, a doctor's office and, quite possibly, a tavern. By a process of elimination, I incline strongly to the belief that this was the Shawen Tavern referred to in the Act of the Legislature.

In the 1831 Act of the Legislature mentioned above, New Town is spoken of as "New Town (Trap)." Somewhere along the line the word "Trap" was added to the name of New Town. The name was spelled in at least two different ways: Trap and Trappe.

I do not know the origin of this addition. There has long been current in Jefferson a legend to the effect that Jefferson was frequently called "Traptown" because it had so many taverns of ill-repute in which the traveler was frequently relieved of his belongings, either by trickery or by force, and that it was not unusual for even some to disappear entirely without a trace. They entered the town at one end, but never left it at the other.

It is quite possible that this legend is founded on fact, but I am rather skeptical of all such legends, and I repeat it here only for whatever it may be worth. My skepticism in this case is furthered by the fact that the

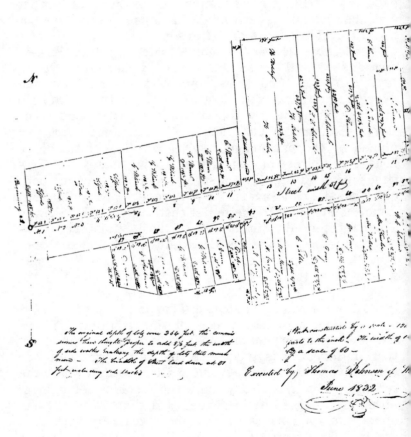

Plat of Jefferson, Maryland as found

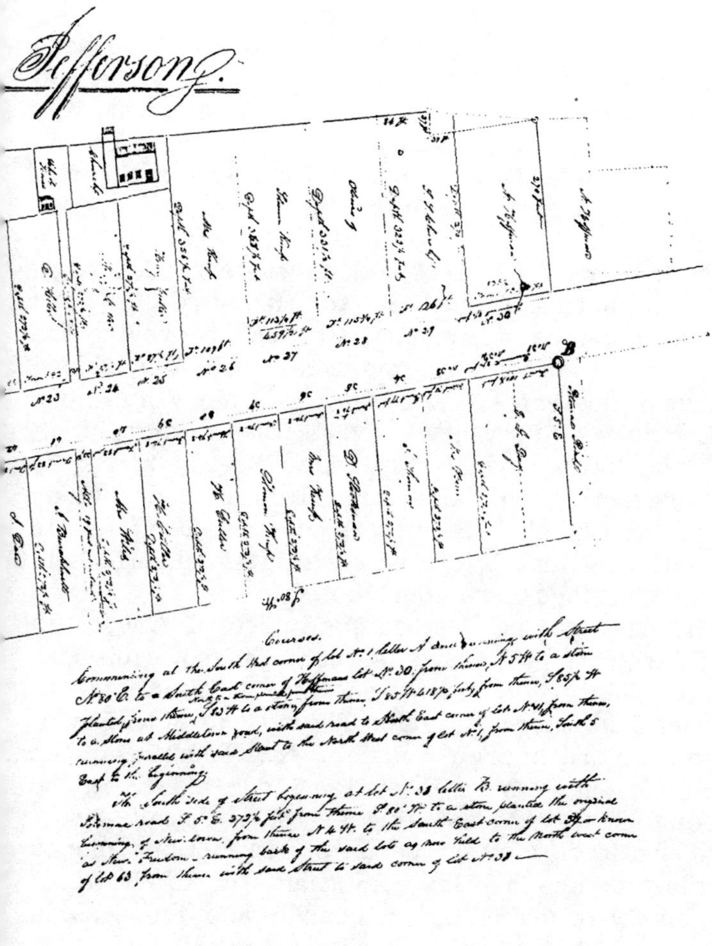

ederick County Land Records, JS39-257.

1794 Dennis Griffith map of Frederick County[37] adds the label "Trap" to New Town, and I doubt that such a small town, whose lots were owned almost exclusively by farmers, could have achieved such a vile reputation only twenty years after its founding.

The history of the churches in Jefferson has been written by the several denominations, and I can add very little here. I'm not certain, however, that it is generally known that a union church, called the Emanuel Church, was erected about 1828 and apparently stood almost directly behind the present Lutheran Church.

On December 17, 1827 a deed was recorded from George Remsburg, trustee, to Henry Culler and others as trustees of Emanuel Church, conveying the plot of ground which now comprises the Reformed and Lutheran Cemeteries.[38] It ran, in other words, behind Lot Nos. 8, 9, 10, 11 and 12 on the old plat of New Town, or behind Lot Nos. 21, 22, 23, 24 and 25 on the present plat of Jefferson. It is my understanding that the church built on this plot was used jointly by the Lutheran and Reformed congregations until their separate churches were constructed.

The deed to the Methodist Episcopal Church is dated March 26, 1838 and is from Eleanor Hoffman, widow of George Hoffman, and his heirs-at-law to Somerset R. Waters, Fielder Thompson, John Ervin, George Rice and Andrew Kessler, Jr., Trustees of the Church.[39] Since there is at least one burial in the Methodist Graveyard as early as 1827, that of James Wiles, and in view of the peculiar restrictions placed upon the trustees by Mrs. Hoffman's deed, it would seem highly probable that a church was there some years before 1838 when the deed was executed.

---

[37] Dennis Griffith, "Map of Maryland" (Philadelphia, 1794); original in Library of Congress.
[38] Frederick County Land Records, JS 28-487.
[39] Ibid., HS 6-367/370. See also below, p. 51.

The further probability exists that George Hoffman may have built the church himself and permitted the congregation to use it before they took title to it. He died in December 1836, and his widow survived him until 1854.

While the building has now been torn down, let me record, because of its historic interest, what rather meagre and sketchy information I have concerning the African Methodist Episcopal Church which stood in the extreme northwest corner of New Town — or, more specifically as to present-day Jefferson, on the Middletown Road behind Lot No. 12 owned in 1975 by Robert E. Houck and north of the dwelling which was until recently the home of Mrs. Charles C. Rhoderick.

This property came into the possession of Charles K. Shaff by deed dated February 26, 1921. His deed is from Richard R. Boston, et al., "trustees of Holland Chapel, M.E. Church of Jefferson," and it recites as the basis for title that the property "has been held and possessed by....Hollins Chapel....from the days of slavery, etc."[40]

I can find no evidence that the original deed to this property was ever recorded. I do find, under date of December 8, 1854, a deed from Henry Nixdorff to Cornelius Cochran conveying Lot Nos. 12 and 13 in Jefferson, "saving and excepting....as much thereof as was heretofore conveyed by....Henry Nixdorff to Absalom P. Kessler and others, being a committee for the purposes expressed therein...."[41] If the committee's purpose was to build a Negro church, this would account for the attempt to establish ownership by right of possession as noted above.

Nixdorff acquired Lot Nos. 12 and 13 on February 26, 1846 from William Mahoney.[42] Hence the deed to Kessler, et al., was made some time between 1846

---

[40] Frederick County Land Records, 335-56.
[41] Ibid., ES5-290.
[42] Ibid., WBT3-107.

and 1854. Apparently the church was built late in 1853, for T. J. C. Williams reported that "a writer complained in January 1854, in a letter to the Frederick Examiner 'that during the past autumn there was erected in the village of Jefferson a church for the sole use of the negroes'." The writer noted that the church was dedicated "about two months ago." He further complained about the demoralizing effect of unsupervised meetings of slaves and of depredations allegedly committed by them when returning home late at night from such church meetings.[43]

I have found nothing in the records concerning education in Jefferson prior to 1841. However, Johnson on his 1832 plat shows a school house situated in what is now the Reformed Cemetery, just west of the mouth of the alley leading to the Cemetery. I know nothing of its history.

In 1841 Andrew Kessler and his wife deeded Lot No. 36 in Jefferson to the Trustees of the Primary School.[44] The purchase price was $60, and the school built there was known as School No. 17. I do not know when a second storey was added to the building, but apparently this was done after it was abandoned as a school about 1897 and was acquired by the Junior Order of United American Mechanics. For many years this fraternal order used the second floor as a lodge room, while the lower part became a community hall. In 1969 the building was razed, and a modern apartment building now occupies the site.

On November 9, 1896 for a consideration of $500 Michael Culler and his wife conveyed to the Board of County School Commissioners of Frederick County an acre of ground at the intersection of the main street and Lander Road.[45] Here a two-room, one-storey

---

[43] T. J. C. Williams and Folger McKinsey, History of Frederick County, Maryland (Hagerstown, Md., L. R. Titsworth, 1910), vol. 1, p. 219.
[44] Frederick County Land Records, HS 13-2.

42

brick school was built, fronting on the main street. A second storey was added later. This building was razed in 1924 and a more modern school building erected immediately behind it. The latter, no longer used as a school, is now owned by the Knights of Columbus. The Valley School, built in 1968, is situated west of Jefferson at Horine Road and serves Jefferson and the surrounding territory.

So far as I can learn, the first movement toward higher education in Jefferson occurred in 1860. On October 9th of that year, Articles of Incorporation were filed for the Jefferson High School Association by George W. Crum, Robert K. Thrasher, Thomas Lamar, Ezra M. Thomas, W. S. Hershperger, Joel Horine and William H. Boteler.[46]

Section 2 of these Articles states that "the object of this association is to establish a high school in the town of Jefferson in Frederick County, Maryland." Section 3 reads as follows: "The capital stock of said company shall consist of not less than $300, nor more than $1,500 — divided in shares of the par value of $5 each."

On March 14, 1861 Cornelius Cochran and his wife deeded to the Jefferson High School Association for a consideration of $40 part of Lot No. 12, adjoining the AME Church on the south and running behind it on the east.[47] There a log building was built. I know little about this institution, but a Professor Sprecher, doubtless among others, taught there in what was, during his time, known as "Professor Sprecher's Academy." This building had been the home of Mrs. Charles C. Rhoderick and was acquired from Charles K. Shaff by deed referred to in the transfer of the AME Church property.

A public high school was established in the early

---

[45] Ibid., JLJ 14-466.
[46] Ibid., BGF 6-198.
[47] Ibid., BGF 6-518.

1900's and existed for a dozen years or more. Since this is relatively modern history and easily available from existing public school records, I have made no effort to supply details here. This school was first held, I believe, in what was then known as Dr. Crum's store room, the west portion of the large brick dwelling recently owned by Charles H. Lewis. It later met — I believe until it was closed — in the abandoned Methodist Protestant Church building at the west end of Jefferson.

Less well known than church and educational history, perhaps, is that of Free-Masonry in New Town. St. Alban's Lodge No. 65 of New Town was first convened in February 1819. It was created from the membership of Columbia Lodge No. 58 of Frederick, and by an order of the Grand Lodge of Maryland dated May 4, 1819, Robert Elliott of Columbia Lodge was directed to install the officers of St. Alban's Lodge.

These first officers were: Dr. Grafton Duvall, Worshipful Master; James S. Hook, Senior Warden; George W. Boastler, Junior Warden. Among the early members were Henry Cost, John Huffer, John Simmons, John Schroder, Samuel Weakely, Nelson Luckette, Perry Spencer, Perry G. Mercer, William B. Chunn, Thomas Keys, John Marlow and Baker Tritt. The records of St. Alban's were last in the possession of Dr. Duvall, and although the Grand Lodge repeatedly asked for their return when the Lodge ceased to function in 1822, they are not in the files of the Grand Lodge of Maryland.

There seems to be nothing in the records to indicate where St. Alban's Lodge held its meetings. Two places are mentioned speculatively. One of these was the old school house which stood in what is now the Reformed Graveyard, just west of the gateway from the alley which leads into the cemetery and almost directly behind the lot on which the Jefferson Bank now stands.

The other probable meeting place, perhaps more frequently used, was in the house then owned by James

Hook, situated between the Point of Rocks and Lander roads overlooking the Potomac River. Still standing following extensive remodeling, it is on the farm recently owned by Mr. Thomas M. Hoffmeister and more familiarly known to older residents as the Abram Hemp farm.

There was in this house a room which is generally believed to have been reserved as a Masonic Lodge Room. It would have been quite logical to hold meetings there, both for secrecy and for the fact that a number of the members lived nearby, notably Hook, Duvall, Luckette, Cost, Simmons and perhaps others.

Now that many of the great trees, mostly maples, which once lined both sides of Jefferson's main street have been removed by the State Roads Commission, it is difficult to realize how well shaded the town once was. For instance, in front of the house where I was born, which stands on a lot of approximately 75 feet frontage, there were five huge maples — all now gone.

My father, who recalled the Civil War quite clearly, having been born in 1844, frequently said that because of its many trees the soldiers of the armies passing through Jefferson called it "The Little Town in the Woods."

Incidentally, the first Mayor of Jefferson after its incorporation was my great grandfather, Captain Henry Culler.

* * * *

Since putting together the above Jefferson material some fifteen years ago, I have come across several bits of information relating to the Town of New Freedom, which I should like to append here.

It was Elias DeLashmutt, Jr., who laid out the town of New Freedom in 1795.[48] At that time the site was a part of CHILDREN'S CHANCE, and its boundaries were quite evidently in dispute. The details of

---

[48] See above, pp. 31-32.

the controversy are difficult to understand and impossible to explain clearly in a brief commentary such as this. It was, however, the reason for the shorter and variable depths of lots south of the road in New Freedom, which I did not show in my plat because I did not then know the reason for it.

The problem apparently arose from the original survey of CHILDREN'S CHANCE. When Thomas Cresap surveyed that tract for Isaac Wells in 1744, he described its beginning point as "at or near the end of the First Line of LOW LAND."[49] Later surveys showed that this point was southwest of the end of the LOW LAND line by eight or ten perches.[50] This created a narrow strip between the two tracts and moved the beginning point southward.

In 1763 Elias DeLashmutt, Jr., had bought the part of CHILDREN'S CHANCE north of the road[51] and Elias, Sr., 120 acres south of the road.[52] The beginning point of the latter was the south side of the road, which was said to be 122 perches from the beginning point of CHILDREN'S CHANCE. When that point was moved southward, 122 perches no longer reached the south side of the road. Before a commission, whose report I do not find, Elias, Jr., successfully claimed this small strip south of the road, and his ownership was confirmed by a resurvey in 1801 resulting in a tract thereafter known as NEW FREEDOM.[53]

I noted above[54] the sale to George Willard by Elias DeLashmutt [Jr.] of Lot No. 6 in New Freedom "adjoining the alley leading to the Spring." I could not indicate this alley in constructing my plat (page 33), since there was no clue to its exact location. I was

---

[49] Prince George's County Patented Certificate #508.
[50] Estimated from map measurements.
[51] Frederick County Land Records, H-454.
[52] Ibid., H-429.
[53] Frederick County Survey Records, THO 2-299.
[54] See above, pp. 31-32.

intrigued by the spring, wondering about its location and whether DeLashmutt intended it to be the source of water for lot buyers in New Freedom. However, his deeds made no mention of privilege to use its waters as, for instance, did early lot deeds in Middletown, which conveyed the right to use the waters "of the springs of the town."

I am now convinced that the New Freedom spring was that spring, which is still flowing, in the meadow of the present Elgin Farm, situated approximately in front of the brick farm house built in 1818 by George Willard who, incidentally, was a son of Elias Willard.

The deed to Willard for Lot No. 6 also conveyed 49 square perches of CHILDREN'S CHANCE situated west of the spring and binding on the boundary of the adjoining property, DANIEL'S DILIGENCE. This deed conveyed to Willard the "right of taking water from the spring to the aforesaid lot."

In a later deed DeLashmutt conveyed on June 4, 1798 an additional 775 square feet to Willard adjoining the above lot, "whereon is a tanyard....which lot was conveyed by Elias DeLashmutt to George Willard...."[55] Therefore, in the three-year interval between these two deeds, George Willard established a tannery which may have been the first industry in the immediate area.

The foregoing leads to a logical explanation (un-verified, however, by anything thus far found in the records) for the beginning point of Christian Sifford's deed to the trustees of the Methodist Protestant Church, which is described as being 10 feet from the line of the adjoining tract, DANIEL'S DILIGENCE.[56]

That ten feet was evidently an alley which DeLash-mutt permitted Willard to use to reach his tannery. (I did not show this on my reconstruction of the plat of New Freedom, for I had then found nothing in the records to suggest an explanation of it.) In 1802 Willard

---

[55] Frederick County Land Records, WR 17-41.
[56] Cf. above, p. 34.

bought from DeLashmutt the part of NEW FREEDOM lying north of the Town and west of Middletown Road. Since his tannery lay within that land, he then had access to it across his own land from that road.

For the benefit of any one who might be interested in identifying the Elias Willard farm, I note here that in his will[57] he devised the land to his son John, but directed that, should the gold mine prove a bonanza, all his children should share equally in the profits.

Estrangement between the Elias DeLashmutts, father and son, is evident. Elias, Sr., in his will cut Elias, Jr., off with a legacy of £5. Moreover, he devised 30 acres of CHILDREN'S CHANCE on which Elias, Jr., had been living to his grandson, Peter DeLashmutt, son of Elias, Jr.[58]

The ultimate effect of this estrangement seems to have been to cause Elias, Jr., and some members of his family to leave Frederick County. In 1808 Elias, Jr., conveyed the thirteen unsold lots in New Freedom to Elias N. DeLashmutt, presumably his son.[59] The latter is shown, in a deed just a few weeks later, to have been living in Franklin County, Ohio.[60]

If Elias DeLashmutt, Sr., ever lived on his part of CHILDREN'S CHANCE, I think it rather obvious that in later years he lived on the land north of Point of Rocks and that he died there, for the witnesses to his will — John Chisholm, Samuel Thomas and Andrew Michael — all lived in that vicinity.

I append four brief pieces relating to Jefferson and its vicinity. Research for them occurred at various times for various purposes, but they may be properly considered as supplementary to the preceding Notes on Jefferson.

---

[57] Frederick County Will Records, HS 2-256.
[58] Ibid., GM 1-37.
[59] Frederick County Land Records, WR 33-438.
[60] Ibid., WR 33-553.

THE TAVERN(?)
AT THE EAST END OF JEFFERSON

Local tradition has it that the old house on the north side of Main Street almost opposite Lander Road in Jefferson, Maryland, was once a tavern.

One of the bases for this tradition is the widely-held belief that beneath the soil in the front yard is a layer of stones, which is thought to indicate that there was once a stone-paved courtyard and that such a yard was typical of many old taverns. Only careful excavation would prove the existence of this layer of stones, and its presence would then be only very circumstantial evidence that the house was once a tavern.

Since there is no known historical reference to this house as a tavern, I have examined the history of the land on which it stands for possible clues.

In 1752 RESURVEY ON WELLS INVENTION was surveyed for Robert Lamar.[1] This tract adjoined Jefferson (New Town) on the east and surrounded it without adjoining it on the north and west. Substantial parts of RESURVEY ON WELLS INVENTION came into the Magruder family of Montgomery County, but very obviously the Magruders were not living on their land. Instead, they were quite probably following a practice of the period whereby large land owners rented to tenants from year to year on a per-acre basis. This arrangement usually required the erection by the landlord of a house for the tenant. Several

---

[1] Frederick County Patented Certificate of Survey #4030. See also below, pp. 60-65.

long-term leases, which are recorded, provide for the erection of "a dwelling 25 x 20 feet with brick or stone chimney."

The house in question is on part of RESURVEY ON WELLS INVENTION. On December 12, 1789 Isaac Magruder of Montgomery County sold to Francis Hoffman for 299 pounds, 5 shillings, 126 acres of RESURVEY ON WELLS INVENTION which, when platted, includes the land on which the house stands and a large part of the farm as now laid out.[2]

Magruder recited in his deed that these 126 acres were part of 500 acres he had acquired about six months previously from Nathan Magruder, Jr., of Montgomery County and further that Magruder, Jr., had inherited this land from his father, Nathan Magruder, Sr., by a will dated January 17, 1781.[3] The latter had purchased these 500 acres from Robert Lamar on November 3, 1757 for £46.[4]

Until very early in this century — possibly about 1902/1904 — a very old log house stood on the north side of the Frederick Road approximately 50 yards east of the house under consideration. In its later years this log building was used as a slaughter-house by John H. Keplinger who sold meats in Jefferson.

This old house was similar in size and construction to many of the early tenant houses described above and may very probably have been used by tenants on the land prior to Hoffman's 1789 purchase.

Francis Hoffman, by the standards of his day, was a man of substantial means. He would quite probably have found this log house unsuited to his needs. It is quite possible, therefore, that he built what is now the back part of the house in question and used the log house for other purposes. There was not sufficient room in that part of the house which I am assuming

---

[2] Frederick County Land Records, WR 8-746.
[3] Montgomery County Record Book, B-239 (1786).
[4] Frederick County Land Records, F-325.

Francis Hoffman built to permit its use as a tavern. Moreover, Hoffman was a farmer and not a tavern-keeper, as his ownership of three or more farms at his death in 1819 well indicates.[5]

In his will Francis Hoffman devised this farm to his son George, who lived on it until his death in 1836. George Hoffman was also a farmer and apparently an actively religious man. In my earlier monograph on Jefferson I speculated that, on the basis of the 1838 deed by George Hoffman's heirs conveying Lot No. 29 in Jefferson to the Methodist Church, he may have built the church or contributed substantially to its cost.[6]

Subsequently I have discovered that he bought the lot in 1832 for $80[7] and his heirs sold it to the Church Trustees for $500,[8] thus indicating the addition of a substantial structure in the interim. The deed of the heirs described the lot, "whereon is erected a stone church."

George Hoffman's religious scruples, therefore, would seem to have precluded his keeping a tavern, even if he was the builder of the front part of the house in question.

In March 1840 George Hoffman's heirs sold the farm to Captain Henry Culler, who was my great-grandfather. Captain Culler was a man of quite substantial means. It was said of him that at one time he could travel from Jefferson to Frederick without getting off his own land. If this statement is only partly true, he was scarcely a man to keep a tavern. It is quite possible, however, that he wanted a more pretentious house than the one on the property in 1840 and that he added the more spacious front part of the house.

---

[5] Frederick County Will Records, HS 2-263.
[6] See above, p. 40.
[7] Frederick County Land Records, JS 42-29.
[8] Ibid., HS 6-367.

Captain Culler died in 1861 and devised this farm to his son David. The land remained in the Culler family for approximately 100 years thereafter, and during that time there were no known tavern keepers in the family.

The foregoing is by no means conclusive evidence, but because of it I cannot convince myself that the house was ever used as a tavern.

EARLY HISTORY OF LEWIS' MILL

The list of owners of what is now known as Lewis' Mill on a small tributary of Catoctin Creek northwest of Jefferson,[1] as given in Williams' History of Frederick County,[2] is essentially correct from 1811 except for the statement that the Mill was built in 1810 by [William] Johnson. The mill is much older than that.

Almost certainly there was a mill at the site long before 1810 and quite probably a number of years before 1778.

On May 20, 1760 Jacob Klyne (Cline) bought 101 acres of ANCHOR AND HOPE from Michael Creager for £100[3] and later acquired additional acreage from that tract and the resurvey on it.

On November 18, 1778 Cline sold 50 acres of RESURVEY ON ANCHOR AND HOPE to Jacob Hoff for £1,500.[4] This deed did not mention a mill, but the price of £30 per acre indicates substantial improvements of some kind. That these improvements included a mill is strongly indicated by Cline's deed of

---

[1] See map, p. 56.

[2] T. J. C. Williams and Folger McKinsey, op. cit., vol. 2, p. 1443. The list of owners of what is there called the Willow Grove Mill included Messrs. [William] Johnson, Schellhouse, Hemp, Henry Culler, Zelophehed Duval, Perry G. Rice, Henry J. Danner, Marcellus Duval and Basil Lewis.

[3] Frederick County Land Records, F-1003.

[4] Ibid., RP 1-539.

April 23, 1784 to Thomas Taylor. By that deed Cline conveyed to Taylor four parcels, parts of ANCHOR AND HOPE and RESURVEY ON ANCHOR AND HOPE, except that part sold to Hoff in 1778 and laid off "with the Mill."[5]

On August 18, 1783 Hoff sold these 50 acres to Valentine Evert "of Washington County, miller."[6] As a miller, Evert was obviously buying a mill.

There was apparently some uncertainty concerning boundary lines, for on October 10, 1790 Evert had a resurvey made which he named THE MILL SEAT SECURED.[7] Then by deed dated June 17, 1811 but not recorded until September 16, 1811 Evert sold 45 acres of THE MILL SEAT SECURED to William Johnson, son of Thomas Johnson, for $2,000.[8]

By another deed dated and recorded on the same days as Evert's deed Johnson sold the same property, together with 20 acres of RESURVEY ON WELLS INVENTION to Peter Shelhouse for £3,350. These identical datings and the difference in considerations are unexplained in anything thus far found in land or other records. The transaction may indicate, however, an addition to the mill, built by Johnson.

---

[5]   Ibid., WR 4-423.
[6]   Ibid., WR 4-149.
[7]   Frederick County Survey Record, HGO 1-456.
[8]   Frederick County Land Records, WR 40-398.

THE ROAD FROM ANTIETAM
TO MOUTH OF MONOCACY
(via Present-day Jefferson)

March Court - 1768
(Liber P-7)[1]

Sixty-five residents of Frederick County petition the Court for relocation of the road "from Christian Orndorff's Mill (on Antietam) to Captain Luckett's Ferry."

They state it "would shorted the road to Markett considerably....It would be much easier for waggons in all seasons of the year then the road....[we] are obliged to travel at present."

The Court appointed the following commissioners to report on a new route: Joseph Smith, James Smith, Christian Orndorff, James Hook.

August Court - 1768
(Liber P-325)[1]

The Commissioners recommended the following route for a road "from Christian Orndorff's Mill on Antietam to the Mouth of Monocacy: From said mill to Peter Hill's plantation, to bridle road gap in Shenadore Mountain; from top of said Mountain to upper side of James Pile's plantation, then to Elias Willyard's and Philip Sylor's, then to cross Kittoctin Creek at a ford below Michael Creager's and to come into the bridle road about three or four hundred yards from a branch below Elias DeLashmutt's, then with said road by De-

---

[1] Frederick County Judgment Records.

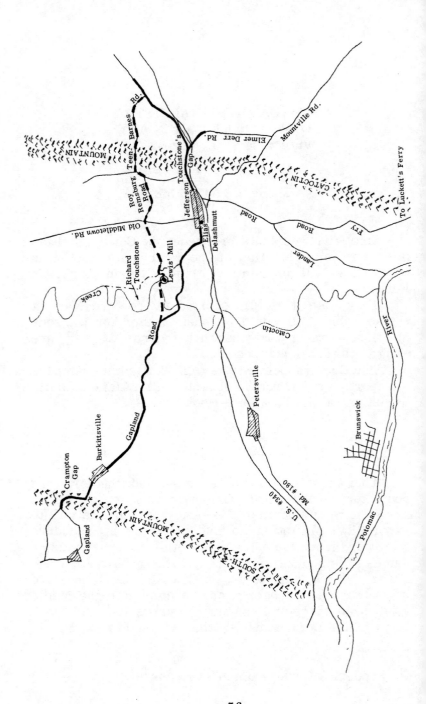

Lashmutt's to a gap in Catoctin Mountain known by the name of Touchstone's Gap, to Mouth of Monocacy."

Some Notes and Speculations on the Foregoing

The Orndorff Mill was almost certainly originally the Israel Friend Mill, though I cannot find in Frederick County Land Records any evidence of Orndorff's ownership. Apparently he acquired the Mill property before 1748. In 1727 Israel Friend received a deed from five tribal Indian Kings for extensive lands on Antietam. Their dimensions were described in "arrow shoots" and the consideration was Love and Affection. [2]

It was on this land that Friend obviously built a mill before 1734, for in that year in a survey for PILE HALL there is reference to the "road to Israel Friend's Mill." Quite probably the road followed an old Indian trail.

The lands of Pile, Willard and Sylor obviously lay east of South Mountain and west of Catoctin Creek. I have made no effort to locate them by present ownership, but it seems almost equally obvious from modern maps that the present road from South Mountain to Jefferson, known variously as the Gapland, Howard Huffer, and Burkittsville-Jefferson Road, follows the general — and perhaps exact — route laid out in the summer of 1768.

This new road very probably caused abandonment as a main road of that part of the old Israel Friend's Mill Road which included present Teen Barnes and Roy Remsburg Roads and perhaps other parts of it also, since its exact route west of Catoctin Creek is unknown, at least to me.

The bridle road described as being entered "below Elias DeLashmutt's" was itself quite old. It was first called Touchstone Road, since it led past Richard Touchstone's land ANCHOR AND HOPE (incorporating

---

[2] Prince George's County Land Records, O-167.

present-day Lewis' Mill), which was surveyed for him in 1739. The beginning point in a 1752 deed conveying part of CHILDREN'S CHANCE was at "the Main Road, commonly called Touchstone Road."[3] In a 1765 deed it was described as the "Main Winchester Road that leads from Frederick Town to Harper's Ferry."[4] Yet as late as 1778 Elias DeLashmutt, Sr., calls it "Tutstone's Road."[5]

The road to Richard Touchstone's turned northward west of Jefferson and was almost certainly that old road, still shown on County maps,[6] which branches off the present Burkittsville-Jefferson Road and leads to Lewis' Mill. Quite possibly the last mile of the new 1768 road, eastbound before it reached today's Md. Route #180, merged into and became a part of it.

The only dwelling landmark mentioned is that of Elias DeLashmutt [Jr.], who lived south of the road but obviously near it. Since he lived on part of CHILDREN'S CHANCE, then owned by Elias DeLashmutt, Sr., his house would have stood between the old Middletown Road and the western end of Jefferson.[7]

The "Touchstone's Gap" mentioned by the commissioners is obviously that gap in Catoctin Mountain through which the Maryland Route 180 and U.S. Route 340 Roads now pass, about a mile east of Jefferson.

From this point the traveler to Mouth of Monocacy had an apparent choice of routes. He could continue on the Frederick Town Road to the vicinity of present Teen Barnes Road and turn southward there. Or he could follow the old road, unnamed on County road maps and now closed, leading through the gap and

---

[3] Frederick County Land Records, B-539.

[4] Ibid., J-1273.

[5] Frederick County Will Records, GM1-37.

[6] E.g., Topographic Map of Frederick County, prepared by the Maryland Geological Survey (rev. 1973).

[7] Frederick County Land Records, H-429; Frederick County Will Records, GM1-37.

southward around the mountain into the Elmer Derr Road.

I have long wondered why the first road from Mouth of Monocacy followed such a difficult route not only in crossing Catoctin Mountain but also in proceeding westward from it. The route through Touchstone Gap led to higher ground and was in general an easier route. Since I think it is obvious that the Israel Friend Road followed an old Indian trail, I have wondered speculatively if, when that trail was made, an unfriendly tribe either occupied or used the Touchstone Gap.

EARLY SURVEYS NEAR JEFFERSON, MARYLAND

For a number of years I have been trying to learn something of the history of RESURVEY ON WELLS INVENTION. My original interest arose from my realization that it surrounded the town of Jefferson on three sides and from my discovery that great great grandfathers on both sides of my family had some contact with it.

William Rice's NEIGHBORS ALARMED had a common boundary with its 32nd and 33rd lines, and Michael Culler acquired 105 acres of it adjoining his MATTHEW'S GOOD WILL.

I later learned that this huge resurvey of 2,017 acres was based on only 92 acres of the original WELLS INVENTION and that the beginning point for both the original and the resurvey was at or near the northeast corner of New Town (Jefferson).

WELLS INVENTION was surveyed on October 27, 1746 for Isaac Wells. He had a Land Office Warrant for 50 acres, and apparently John Cholmondley paid for the additional 42 acres. There is no evidence as to the relationship, business or otherwise, between Wells and Cholmondley, but on March 9, 1750 a warrant for the whole tract was issued to Cholmondley.[1]

Wells had died about 1747,[2] and on September 2, 1751 Ann Dunbar, describing herself as the wife of David Dunbar and the widow of Isaac Wells, executed in

---

[1] Prince George's County Unpatented Certificate of Survey #382.
[2] Prince George's County Will Records, 25-61/63.

North Carolina a release of her dower in LOW LAND.[3]

John Cholmondley apparently died on May 14, 1752, for his will is dated on that day and was probated on the following day.[4] He made two small cash bequests and left all his other property, real and personal, to Robard [Robert] Lamar, Jr., whom he named as executor.

Lamar had a resurvey made on the 92 acres of WELLS INVENTION, which resulted in the 2,017 acres of RESURVEY ON WELLS INVENTION. This was patented to him on August 10, 1753.[5] Apparently all of the 1,925 acres added to the original 92 acres was vacant land. This was a surprisingly large acreage of vacancy to be annexed by resurvey — the largest in Frederick County of which I have any knowledge. Because surveys had been made in the general area since 1734, it seems strange that at least some of this vacancy had not been surveyed. I have discussed this with several local historians, but none of them can offer an explanation.

Through the kindness of Mr. Frank W. Rothenhoefer, Sr., I came into possession of the outline survey of the RESURVEY ON WELLS INVENTION (see heavy lines on page 62). As I studied the early surveys surrounding or forming parts of Jefferson, I undertook to plat them. As a result of these plattings I realized that their relationship to Jefferson and to each other could be shown rather clearly by placing them in position on the RESURVEY ON WELLS INVENTION plat. This I have tried to do with sufficient accuracy to satisfy the layman, if not the engineer.

---

[3] Frederick County Land Records, B-471. LOW LAND, which lay to the west of WELLS INVENTION, had been acquired by Wells in 1741 (Prince George's County Land Records, Y-403/406).

[4] Frederick County Will Records, A1-76.

[5] Frederick County Patented Certificate of Survey #4030.

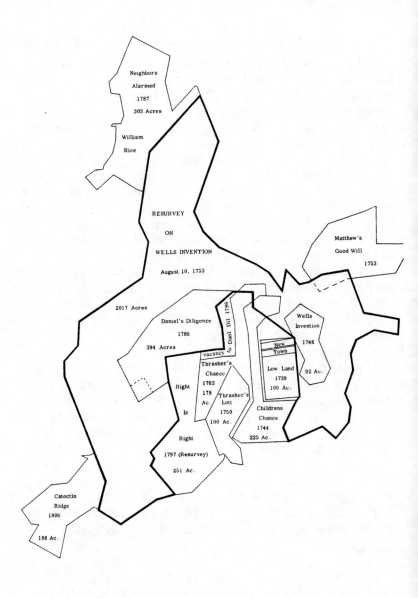

Early Surveys Near Jefferson, Maryland

62

For whatever interest and value it may have for genealogists and other researchers, I recount below what I know of the several surveys and resurveys shown on the plat.

With respect to LOW LAND, the earliest survey shown, there is little to be added to what I have noted in my Jefferson sketch[6] I have never found an explanation for the slight encroachment on it at its northeast corner as indicated on the 1832 plat of Jefferson.[7] Since LOW LAND predated other contiguous surveys, its boundaries should not have been disturbed by those later surveys.

CHILDREN'S CHANCE was surveyed in 1744 for Isaac Wells, who at that time also owned LOW LAND.[8] Elsewhere I have discussed at some length the vicissitudes of this tract.[9]

THRASHER'S LOT was an original survey in 1750 for Thomas Thrasher.[10] So also was THRASHER'S CHANCE, surveyed in 1763.[11] I have been mystified by the peculiar outlines, especially at the north, of the latter and of CHILDREN'S CHANCE which it adjoins. So far as I know there were no earlier surveys which made these odd shapes necessary. Nor have I been able to understand the encroachment of THRASHER'S CHANCE on the RESURVEY ON WELLS INVENTION, which was the older survey by approximately ten years. Conversely, I can find no explanation for the encroachment of the latter on CHILDREN'S CHANCE, which was the older survey by nine years.

In 1765 Thrasher sold to James Hook the 78 acres

---

[6] See above, pp. 20-27.
[7] Ibid., pp. 38-39.
[8] Prince George's County Patented Certificate of Survey #508.
[9] See above, pp. 45-46.
[10] Prince George's County Patented Certificate of Survey #4767.
[11] Frederick County Patents BC & GS #23-39/40.

of THRASHER'S CHANCE which lay north of the Harper's Ferry Road.[12] The remainder, together with THRASHER'S LOTT, was resurveyed for Thrasher in 1797 into one tract of 224 acres called ENOUGH AND TO SPARE, on which he was living at the time of his death in 1804.[13]

RIGHT IS RIGHT is a resurvey containing 251 acres, made in 1797 for Jacob Cost.[14] It was composed of parts of WIDOW'S REST, COST'S GOOD LUCK, and FIELDEREA. The latter contained 9,151 acres. WIDOW'S REST was a very old survey of 100 acres made in 1746 for William Matthews, who sold it in 1755 to Jacob Cost's father, Francis Cost.[15] It had a common beginning point with THRASHER'S LOTT and formed its southwestern boundary. As platted here, RIGHT IS RIGHT is somewhat enlarged and distorted because of my force-fitting it into the surrounding boundaries.

I have shown only the western and northern boundaries of DANIEL'S DILIGENCE in order to avoid a maze of overlapping lines on this small scale plat. It was a resurvey of 394 acres made in 1786 for James Hook and was composed of 78 acres of THRASHER'S CHANCE and 300 acres of RESURVEY ON WELLS INVENTION, plus some contiguous vacancy.[16] The tract was named for Hook's son Daniel, to whom he gave it in 1789.[17] The square shown in the southwest corner of the tract represents 12 acres sold by Daniel to John Cain in 1797.[18] In 1799 Daniel Hook sold his land to

---

[12] Frederick County Land Records, J-1273. Harper's Ferry Road was the westward extension of Main Street in New Town.
[13] Frederick County Survey Records, THO 1-68; Frederick County Will Records, GMRB 1-31.
[14] Frederick County Survey Records, THO 1-133.
[15] Frederick County Land Records, E-693.
[16] Frederick County Survey Records, HGO 1-139.
[17] Frederick County Land Records, WR 8-742.

William Johnson[19] and in a power of attorney executed in April, 1800, indicated his intention to move to Kentucky.[20]

I have not shown either the tract NEW FREEDOM or the town of New Freedom laid out on part of it by Elias DeLashmutt, Jr. My reason for this omission was again to avoid, on this small-scale plat, a maze of lines which could be confusing and perhaps unintelligible. Moreover, different surveys and deeds recite differing courses and distances, so that the tract's exact boundaries are somewhat debatable.

However, the NEW FREEDOM tract was composed essentially of the narrow strip of land along the west side of LOW LAND and the land north of the Harper's Ferry Road inclosed by the western and northern lines of CHILDREN'S CHANCE and the closing line of RE-SURVEY ON WELLS INVENTION. I have been unable to determine how DeLashmutt acquired the land on which he laid out the lots of New Freedom town on the south side of the Harper's Ferry Road.

---

[18] Ibid., WR 15-489.
[19] Ibid., WR 19-222.
[20] Ibid., WR 19-440.

JOHN HANSON'S REAL ESTATE TRANSACTIONS
IN FREDERICK COUNTY, MARYLAND

John Hanson, born at Mulberry Grove in Charles County, Maryland on April 13, 1721, removed to Frederick County in late 1772 or early 1773. He was one of those Maryland patriots active in the cause of independence from England and, when that was achieved, in the adoption of the Articles of Confederation. He is frequently called "the first President of the United States" because on November 5, 1781 he was chosen by the Congress as its President for the first term prescribed in the recently ratified Articles. The Presidency, which was for a term of one year, was more ceremonial than executive and not unlike that of the present Vice President, whose chief constitutional function is to serve as President of the Senate.

While the State of Maryland chose John Hanson and Charles Carroll to represent it in Statuary Hall in the Captiol, chroniclers have not given Hanson a very prominent place in the nation's history. This is due in part, perhaps, to the nature of the office and to the fact that Hanson was only one of several "Presidents of the United States in Congress Assembled" — the names of the others being known chiefly to historians.[1] Hanson died in 1783, and his burial place is unknown.

Several reasons are given for Hanson's removal to Frederick County, chief of which was that he might stimulate in Frederick County the sentiment for independence. Since the Stamp Act had been repudiated in

---

[1] See Special Note, p. 77.

Frederick County seven years before Hanson moved there, this seems somewhat like carrying coals to Newcastle. Some historians believe that Hanson's chief interest in Frederick County lay in the opportunity for land speculation and that he was greatly influenced in this by his friendship with Richard Potts, himself a land speculator. Whatever Hanson's reasons, once he became a resident of the County, he did develop an active interest in Frederick County real estate.

The following listing, while of interest in itself, was undertaken for a specific purpose. In view of Hanson's social and financial background, I could not shake the doubt that he would have been content to live in the obviously modest house he purchased in Frederick Town. Because of that doubt I began a search for a possible country estate on which he might have lived — at least in the summer months. For that purpose I examined every recorded real estate transaction in which Hanson was involved.

As is obvious in the following record, I paid particular attention to the price paid for rural tracts and their ultimate selling prices. My purpose was to find, if possible, the purchase or lease of an obviously valuable or pretentious property. If I had found a property purchased at a relatively modest price but ultimately sold at a much higher price, my conclusion would have been that it had been extensively improved by Hanson for his own occupancy. The record discloses no such transaction. And when allowance is made for normal increase in property values, no property held for any length of time was sold at any great profit. I conclude, therefore, that none of John Hanson's rural land purchases or leases ever became a country estate.

Hanson's first purchase of land in Frederick County was by two deeds dated December 4, 1772, whereby he acquired Lots 28 and 21 in Frederick Town from Adam Simon Kuhn (also Coon, Coone) of Lancaster County, Pennsylvania.[2] Daniel Dulany had first sold Lot No. 28 to Michael Stump on July 13, 1753 for £5,[3] and on March 29, 1763 Kuhn had purchased the lot from Stump for £100.[4] Kuhn had acquired Lot No. 21 from Dulany's son on June 18, 1772 for £5.[5] In his 1772 purchase Hanson paid Kuhn £315 for Lot No. 28 and £100 for Lot No. 21. Lot No. 28 now comprises Nos. 106 and 108 West Patrick Street in Frederick City. Lot No. 21 lay directly behind Lot No. 28 and extended across Carroll Creek to West All Saint's Street.

The purchase price for Lot No. 28 would indicate the presence thereon of a modest dwelling which, from later evidence, was replaced by a new one built between 1800 and 1812 on the west one-half of the Lot. This would presently be 108 West Patrick Street, which until recently was popularly believed to have been Hanson's home from shortly after he acquired it until his death in 1783. My reasons for disagreeing with this belief were set forth in a special report to the John Hanson House Restoration Committee in 1971. A copy of that report is appended below. (See p. 75.)

Hanson's two deeds of December 4, 1772 were not recorded until April 14, 1773. On that same day there was also recorded a lease, dated in 1772, from William Luckett to John Hanson and Thomas Contee.[6] The lease was for the lifetime of the survivor of the three parties thereto, and the consideration was a yearly rent of one penny. It conveyed to Contee and Hanson, "merchants," one lot 60 x 60 feet, "lying near the store-house where....[they] now keep store, being near the dwelling house of....William Luckett....on which Lott....the said Contee and Hanson are about to build a warehouse...."

---

[2] Frederick County Land Records, P-696, P-698.
[3] Ibid., E-230.
[4] Ibid., H-348.
[5] Ibid., P-164.
[6] Ibid., P-686.

There is nothing in the lease which identifies the land so leased or the location of the Contee-Hanson store and warehouse. Luckett owned various parcels of land, but his principal holding was 498 acres of MEREDITH'S HUNTING QUARTERS, situated near the mouth of the Monocacy River, which Luckett bought from the estate of Meredith Davis, Sr., in 1755. This could be the unproved basis of speculation that the Contee-Hanson store was near the mouth of the Monocacy.

A non-real estate transaction of May 4, 1773[7] may have been in connection with the Contee and Hanson merchandising. This was a chattel mortgage in the form of a bill of sale from George Walker to Contee and Hanson which pledged a horse valued at £10 and bedding and furniture, also valued at £10, for a debt of £20.

Beginning on September 3, 1774, Hanson's real estate transactions quickened. On that date he bought from Basil Beall 85 acres of RESURVEY ON ADDITION TO HAZEL THICKET for 28 Pounds, 16 shillings.[8] And on February 11, 1775, he bought, also from Beall, 38½ acres of RESURVEY ON LIMESTONE ROCK.[9] These tracts, which apparently adjoined, were west of the village of Feagaville, north of today's Maryland Route #180, and in the general vicinity of present Teen Barnes Road. Teen Barnes Road was a part of the very early Israel Friend's Mill Road from the Mouth of Monocacy to Antietam. (See pp. 55-59.)

Hanson acquired 100 acres of EPINAH from Daniel Dulany on December 18, 1775.[10] The consideration here was Hanson's surrender to Dulany of Dulany's bond of £170 to John Holm, which Holm had assigned to Hanson. EPINAH lay approximately west of Mt.

---

7   Ibid., S-207.
8   Ibid., BD 1-86.
9   Ibid., BD 1-529.
10 Ibid., BD 2-279.

Zion Lutheran Church, near Feagaville, adjacent to Lot No. 14 of FIELDEREA.[11]

On his next transaction, Hanson realized a rather quick and substantial profit. On August 8, 1777, he bought from James Brand two lots "on the west side of Frederick Town."[12] The purchase price was £590. On March 10, 1778, Hanson sold these lots to George Snyder for £1,100.[13] These lots were described as "where said Brand lately lived" and as having been "formerly laid out for a certain Sylas Enyhart."

Their point of beginning was "a stone about 3 yards from the west end of a bridge." From that point their front line ran S72°W 181½ feet, then S11°E 268½ feet in depth. The lots are identifiable on the original Frederick Town plat as that unnumbered and unlabeled parallelogram of land fronting on the south side of West Patrick Street, with its northwest corner at the intersection of Patrick and Bentz Streets. The bridge, obviously, spanned Carroll Creek.

At least two more of Hanson's transactions were leases. On October 23, 1778, he leased from Daniel Dulany's agent, Joshua Testill, 150 acres of LOCUST LEVEL.[14] The lease was for 14 years, with a yearly rental of £30. The terms required Hanson to build a dwelling 25 x 20 feet in dimensions, "with brick or stone chimney" and to "keep in good repair the barn now erected thereon."

It is of some interest to note that on the same day, Hanson's son-in-law, Dr. Philip Thomas, leased 104¼ acres of LOCUST LEVEL for 14 years at £20 yearly rental, and by the terms of his lease was required to build a house similar to Hanson's, and also a barn.[15] LOCUST LEVEL lay principally south of Frederick

---

[11]   Ibid., JWLC 4-92.
[12]   Ibid., RP-310.
[13]   Ibid., WR 1-50.
[14]   Ibid., WR 1-342.
[15]   Ibid., WR 1-406.

Town and east of present Maryland Route #355.

On July 16, 1779 Hanson leased from Dulany for 14 years 105 acres, being part of ALBION'S [ALBIN'S] CHOICE and of SPRING GARDEN.[16] Yearly rental was £28. Hanson was required to build a house similar to that on LOCUST LEVEL, and also a barn. There is no doubt concerning the location of ALBIN'S CHOICE, which was in the vicinity of the present Frederick City Airport, and in part, at least, now occupied by it. There was also a SPRING GARDEN in that vicinity. However, the 1866 deed noted above[17] refers to EPINAH SPRING GARDEN and it is possible, therefore, that the SPRING GARDEN of the 1779 lease was in the vicinity of EPINAH.

The most ambitious and, potentially at least, the most profitable of Hanson's real estate ventures was that involving the tract at the northeast corner of West Patrick and Bentz Streets. On Samuel Duvall's 1782 Plat of Frederick Town[18] this tract is labeled "Sundrie Lots Sold by Messrs. Hanson and Potts." Hanson's deed to this property cannot be found in the Frederick County Land Records. Hence, the purchase price is unknown. However, in his deeds selling lots into which the tract was divided, he recited that this was land "sold by Benjamin Dulany to John Hanson." And, whatever his financial relationship to Richard Potts, Hanson alone executed the deeds.

The above may have been a joint venture with Potts and Dr. Philip Thomas, for in his will of September 20, 1781, probated April 13, 1784,[19] Hanson directed that the unsold lots be sold and the proceeds be divided equally between Potts, Dr. Thomas and

---

[16] Ibid., WR 2-207.
[17] Ibid., JWLC 4-92.
[18] George H. Shafer's 1876 copy of this plat hangs presently on the wall in the public meeting room at the City Hall of Frederick.
[19] Frederick County Will Records, GM 2-75.

Hanson's estate. His will devised all his property, real and personal, to his widow, Jane Contee Hanson, for life and named his son, Alexander Contee Hanson, as residuary legatee. The two unsold lots were Nos. 6 and 9, which were sold in 1784 by his heirs.

There is a 1781 plat of this tract recorded,[20] which purports to show it divided into ten lots of varying shapes and sizes, all fronting on the north side of West Patrick Street. However, comparison of this plat with that shown on the Town Plat is more confusing than helpful (see accompanying map, p. 73). Deeds conveying eight of these lots, Nos. 3 to 10 inclusive, showing sale prices, are recorded in Frederick County Land Records as follows:

#3	WR 2-615	Apr. 7, 1780	to Valentine Shriner	£805
#4-5	WR 2-423	Feb. 18, 1780	to Francis Mantz	1,238
#6*	WR 5-181	Apr. 21, 1784	to Bartholemeu McCann	100
#7	WR 2-576	Apr. 7, 1780	to Conrad Doll	610
#8	WR 2-507	Apr. 7, 1780	to George Bear	755
#9*	WR 4-438	Apr. 21, 1784	to Daniel Hower	60
#10	WR 2-493	Apr. 7, 1780	to George Brengle	600

The total of the sale prices for the eight lots was: £4,168
* These sales were by Jane C. and Alexander C. Hanson.

Two of Hanson's above deeds, conveying Lot Nos. 7 and 8, recite that these lots were "sold at auction." Two other deeds, dated the same day and conveying Lot Nos. 3 and 10, make no mention of sale at auction. The presumption is strong, however, that all four lots were thus sold. Lot Nos. 4 and 5 were sold on February 18, 1780, and quite possibly, with no other immediate prospects for private sale, Hanson decided on an auction for all four sold on April 7, 1780. Lot Nos. 6 and 9 were then still unsold and remained so at his death. Their disposition was as shown above.

There is nothing in the records to indicate what happened to Hanson's leased lands after his death in 1783. The two leases listed above had approximately nine and ten years to run, and if the specified build-

---

[20] Frederick County Land Records, WR 2-915.

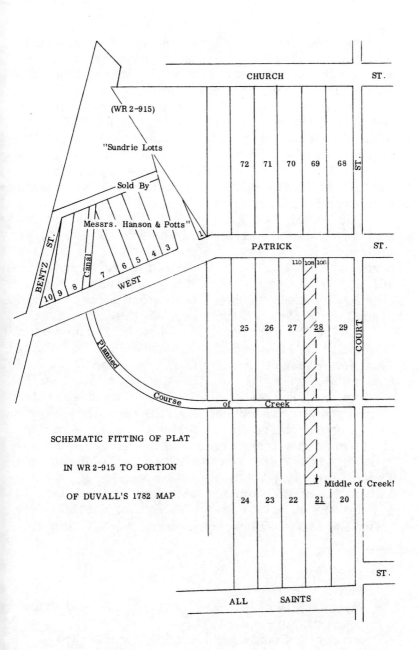

CHURCH ST.

(WR 2-915)

"Sundrie Lotts

Sold By

Messrs. Hanson & Potts"

BENTZ ST.
Canal
WEST
Planned
Course
of Creek

72 71 70 69 68
ST.

PATRICK ST.

110 108 106

25 26 27 28 29
COURT

Middle of Creek!

SCHEMATIC FITTING OF PLAT

IN WR 2-915 TO PORTION

OF DUVALL'S 1782 MAP

24 23 22 21 20

ST.

ALL SAINTS

73

ings had been built, they represented a considerable investment. There is no evidence, however, indicating whether the leases were sold or the leased lands and improvements reverted to Dulany.

On January 14, 1785, Alexander Contee Hanson and his wife Rebecca, both "of Anne Arundel County" (i.e., of Annapolis), sold to Adam Ramsburg the 100 acres of EPINAH which John Hanson had acquired in 1775. The sale price was £300. Jane Contee Hanson, John Hanson's widow, did not join in this deed in order to release her life interest.[21]

The last of John Hanson's rural land holdings was sold on January 10, 1793 to Louis Jean St. Martin de Bellevue, a Frenchman, for £300.[22] This was the parts of RESURVEY ON HAZEL THICKET and RESURVEY ON LIMESTONE ROCK (cf. p. 69). The sale was by Alexander Contee Hanson and Rebecca, and again Jane Hanson did not join in the deed.

In 1798 the west one-half of Lot No. 28 and part of Lot No. 21 in Frederick Town were sold to Dr. Philip Thomas, Hanson's son-in-law, by Alexander Contee Hanson.[23] On April 30, 1813 the latter also sold the east one-half of Lot No. 28 and the remainder of Lot No. 21 to John Hanson Thomas, the son of Dr. Thomas.[24] Shortly thereafter, on May 4, 1813, John Hanson Thomas then transferred title to the part of Lot No. 21 south of Carroll Creek to his father.[25] John Hanson Thomas died May 2, 1815, and on August 28, 1836 his widow, Mary I. Thomas, sold the remaining parts of Lot Nos. 28 and 21 to Joseph Talbott for $3,150, executing the deed in Berkeley County, West Virginia.[26]

---

[21] Ibid., WR 5-493.

[22] Ibid., WR 11-639.

[23] Ibid., WR 16-233. See above, p. 67, and below, my report of November 1971.

[24] Frederick County Land Records, WR 44-255.

[25] Ibid., WR 44-336.

[26] HS 3-439.

REPORT TO THE HANSON HOUSE
RESTORATION COMMITTEE

It was suggested at the meeting of the John Hanson House Restoration Committee on October 10, 1971 that I be asked to look further into the ownership and other facts concerning the west one-half of Lot No. 28, this being 108 West Patrick Street. The following are my findings to date.

As Mrs. Kreitzer[1] has already reported, John Hanson purchased Lot No. 28 from Adam Kuhn on December 4, 1772.[2] The purchase price was 315 Pounds. On the same day Hanson also bought Lot No. 21 from Kuhn for 100 Pounds.[3]

The purchase price of Lot No. 28 may indicate the presence on the lot of a modest dwelling, but scarcely one which a man of John Hanson's social and financial background would care for long to occupy as his residence.

In his will, dated September 20, 1781 and probated April 13, 1784,[4] John Hanson devised all his real property to his wife, Jane Contee Hanson, for her lifetime, providing that at her death it should descend to his son, Alexander Contee Hanson. Part of the real estate, of course, was Lot No. 28. On January 20, 1798 Alexander Contee Hanson and his wife Rebecca conveyed the west one-half of Lot No. 28 to Dr. Philip Thomas, John Hanson's son-in-law, who lived on Lot No. 27, which adjoined Lot No. 28 on the west and is now known as 110 West Patrick Street.[5]

The part of Lot No. 28 conveyed to Dr. Thomas was described as follows: Beginning on Patrick Street at "the northwest corner of Lot No. 28, the same being

---

[1] Mrs. Teri Kreitzer, member of the Committee.
[2] Frederick County Land Records, P-696.
[3] Ibid., P-698.
[4] Frederick County Wills, GM2-75.
[5] Frederick County Land Records, WR16-233.

a northeast corner of Dr. Philip Thomas' dwelling house, and running with Patrick Street east 30 feet, 6 inches; thence down the said lot a line parallel to the dividing line between Lots 28 and 27, 585 feet into Lot 21 and to the middle of the creek....running through Lot 21, thence through the creek west to the exterior line of Lot 21, and thence with that and the corresponding line of Lot 28 north to the beginning...." The consideration for this property was 155 Pounds, which was slightly less than half the cost of the whole lot in 1772 and which raises the question whether the house had either been destroyed or was considered valueless as a dwelling.

And then, on September 13, 1800, Dr. Thomas deeded this half-lot to his son, John Hanson Thomas, the consideration being Love and Affection.[6] This may have been a coming-of-age gift from father to son, for John Hanson Thomas was born May 8, 1779.

Dr. Thomas died April 25, 1815. In his will, dated June 5, 1812 and probated June 23, 1815, he devised to John Hanson Thomas certain property "in addition to the parts of lots in Frederick Town already given by deed to my said son on which I have since built him a house."[7] Since I can find only the one deed (above) from father to son, it seems obvious that the will refers to the west one-half of Lot. No. 28.

Mrs. Kreitzer has already noted John Hanson Thomas' purchase of the east one-half of Lot No. 28 (106 West Patrick Street) on April 30, 1813 and the sale of the whole Lot on August 28, 1836 by John's widow, Mary I. Thomas.

In his will, Dr. Thomas described his own dwelling as "the two-story brick house in which I now live in Frederick Town...." From the deed of September 13, 1800[8] it is shown that the east wall of his house

---

6   Ibid., WR 20-170.
7   Frederick County Wills, HS 1-27.   My underline.
8   Frederick County Land Records, WR 20-170.

was on the line between Lot Nos. 28 and 27.

By way of passing, though tragic, interest, John Hanson Thomas died, according to his tombstone, of "illness contracted at the bedside of his father, who died six days before him."

All of the foregoing seems quite definitely to indicate that the dwelling on the west one-half of Lot No. 28, now known as 108 West Patrick Street, was built after September 13, 1800 — although possibly on the foundation of an earlier structure.

Millard Milburn Rice
November 1971

------

[8] Frederick County Land Records, WR 20-170.

SPECIAL NOTE

I am indebted to Mr. John P. Dern, Redwood City, California, for the following list of Presidents serving under the Articles of Confederation:

Samuel HUNTINGTON was President of the Congress when on March 1, 1781 the Articles were finally ratified. He stayed on without any question of change, but on July 6th asked to be relieved because of his health.

Samuel JOHNSTON of North Carolina was chosen President on July 9, 1781. He declined the next day.

Thomas McKEAN of Delaware was elected on July 10, 1781. On October 19th Cornwallis surrendered. The news reached Philadelphia on October 22nd, and McKEAN was aroused from his slumber to hear that news. Although Washington's official word did not arrive until October 24th, on October 23rd McKEAN, who had originally planned to serve only to October, offered to resign in order to pave the way for election of a new President. Congress accepted his resignation and set the next day for the election. On that

October 24th John Witherspoon reminded the Congress that the Articles specified a "Federal Year" for which the President was to be elected. It was to begin on the first Monday of November. He urged McKEAN to stay on until an election on that day, and McKEAN and Congress agreed.

John HANSON was elected President on November 5, 1781 (Monday) to serve that first prescribed term. Thus he was not the first to serve under the Confederation, nor as the first President of the Congress. But his was the first term as specified by the Articles.

Elias BOUDINOT of New Jersey was elected for the second term, beginning on November 4, 1782.

Thomas MIFFLIN of Pennsylvania was elected for the third term, beginning on November 3, 1783.

Richard Henry LEE was elected on November 30, 1784, as problems of obtaining quorums delayed his election and began to raise questions whether the Confederation could continue.

John HANCOCK, although not present, was elected in late 1785, but he never served. David Ramsay of South Carolina was chairman during his absence.

Nathaniel GORHAM was elected on June 6, 1786, following HANCOCK's resignation on June 5th. There was no meeting of the Congress from November 3, 1786 to January 17, 1787, and even on the latter date no President could be chosen for want of a quorum.

Arthur ST. CLAIR of Pennsylvania was finally elected on February 2, 1787, but assemblage of a quorum remained a problem.

Cyrus GRIFFIN of Virginia was elected on January 22, 1788 as the last President while the days of the Confederation drew to a close.

SOME NOTE RELATIVE TO THE CULLER FAMILY, DESCENDANTS OF JACOB AND MARY KOLLER[1]

This is not a history of the Culler Family. My efforts in connection with the family story have been directed primarily toward two ends: (1) to correct a considerable number of errors and inaccuracies in what has been written by various members of the family and (2) to undertake to learn something of the progenitors of the family older than any heretofore (so far as I can learn) known and recorded by others.

The Cullers of Maryland, and those who migrated from Maryland to Ohio, consider Michael Culler as their oldest known ancestor. They are not so sure what Michael's wife's name was. My Uncle Millard F. Culler, in his biographical sketch in the History of Frederick County,[2] states that Michael's wife was a Miss Rinehart. Another Uncle, the Rev. Martin L. Culler, in a sketch written in the 1920's states that her name was Maria Smith.

Actually, her name was Eleanor Smith, daughter of Jacob and Catherine Smith. There is ample proof of this in the records of the Clerk of the Circuit Court of Frederick County, Maryland. In the "Book of Descents" it is shown that Eleanor Smith was the eldest

---

[1] The charts, maps and other exhibits on pp. 110-126 are an integral part of this sketch. Reference thereto is essential to a clear understanding of the text.

[2] T. J. C. Williams and Folger McKinsey, History of Frederick County, Maryland (Hagerstown, L. R. Titsworth, 1910), vol. 2, p. 1085.

daughter of Jacob Smith and the wife of Michael Koller (Culler), that Jacob Smith died December 6, 1805, intestate, possessed of 141 acres of land, and that his wife had pre-deceased him.[3]   In the Land Records Eleanor Smith is again shown as the deceased wife of Michael Culler.[4]   And in an earlier deed it is shown that Jacob Smith's wife was Catherine.[5]

In the original Lutheran Church records[6] it is shown that on July 7, 1772 Johann Michael Koller, unmarried and legitimate son of Jacob Koller, married Eleonora Schmidin, unmarried and legitimate daughter of Jacob Schmid, both living in Frederick County. In the Land Records under date of April 11, 1806 is recorded a deed from "Leonora Culler" to "Michael Culler, Her husband," the consideration being "love and affection....also....5 shillings...."[7] This instrument conveys to Michael all her interest in the lands of "my father, Jacob Smith....who died intestate," and then lists the names of the several tracts.

The latter deed and its date give rise to an interesting speculation about Eleanor's health. According to her two tombstones in the Culler family graveyard, Eleanor died May 28, 1806, just 47 days after the execution of the deed. Rather obviously, therefore, she was in failing health on April 11th, and this deed was made in anticipation of death. Under the laws of inheritance in Maryland, if she had died intestate, Michael would have received only a third interest in Eleanor's interest in her father's lands, and the other

---

[3] "Docket Commissions under the Act to Direct Descents, 1786-1820," pp. 122 et seq. Frederick Court House.

[4] Frederick County Land Records, WR 29-450.

[5] Ibid., B-36.

[6] Untitled original Frederick Lutheran Church Book, p. 361; at the Lutheran Theological Seminary Library, Gettysburg, Pennsylvania.

[7] Frederick County Land Records, WR 29-136.

80

two-thirds would have vested undivided in his eight children. Her deed vested all her interest in Michael.

With all of the foregoing evidence in the public records — there may be still more I have not found — it seems rather strange to me that there should ever have been any doubt or confusion who Michael's wife was.

But the marriage record of Michael and Eleanor contains some other very interesting information. It tells us who Michael's father was — something which heretofore some of the family historians seem not to have known. His mother's name was Mary Magdalena. She is called Mary in the 1767/68 land records, [8] but Magdalena in a 1755 baptism record[9] and Magdalin in a 1774 deed. [10] Her death is not recorded, but obviously occurred before August 19, 1775 when Jacob Koller, widower, married as his second wife Maria Magdalena Abelin, widow. [11]

What, then, of Jacob Culler? The variation in spelling — Keller, Koller, Collar, Collier, Coller, etc. — of what is now Culler in Maryland and parts of Ohio, but Cullers in Virginia and Missouri, is a serious and confusing handicap to the search of early records. Most of the indexing for Jacob in the early Frederick County records is as Jacob Keller, as I have shown in the lists of land transactions below. [12]

As evidenced by the purchase of 102 acres of RAMSHORN, Jacob first appears in the records of Frederick County in 1750, as Jacob Keller. Thus far, I have been unable to learn where he came from or anything else about him prior to that time. It is my hope that if I am unable in my lifetime to learn some-

---

[8] See below, pp. 114, 116.
[9] Frederick Lutheran Church Book, loc. cit., p. 11.
[10] Frederick County Land Records, V-516. See also below, p. 116.
[11] Frederick Lutheran Church Book, loc. cit., p. 370.
[12] See below, pp. 114, 116.

thing about him before 1750, with what I have set down herein as a starting point, some interested descendant of Jacob may succeed where I fail.

I think that from 1750 to 1754 — and perhaps longer — Jacob and his family may have lived on RAMSHORN, about a mile south of present-day Myersville. This belief is bolstered by his 1787 deed from Shenandoah County, Virginia, transferring Lot #13 in Myers' Addition to Frederick City to his son, John.[13] Note what he says about his "trusty friend Lawrence Delauter."

Delauter and his wife Barbara owned land near or adjoining RAMSHORN, as evidenced by their deed dated March 22, 1773,[14] conveying to Christopher Brown 50 acres of AGREED IN TIME, "situated on the east side of a run called Mill Run above [?] the falls." Mill Run, now known as Little Catoctin Creek, flows a mile or more east of RAMSHORN. Quite probably Jacob and Delauter were close neighbors.

This 1750 date raises some interesting questions. The descendants of Michael Culler have always pointed to the register of the ship "Peggy" which arrived in Philadelphia October 16, 1754, wherein is listed one Michael Köller.[15] On the basis of that record, they have believed that Michael, born in 1745, came to America as a boy of nine to join his father. Actually that register lists only adults, but no wives, children or ages.

Moreover, if Michael's father owned land here as early as 1750, it is scarcely likely he would have waited until 1754 to send for his (probably eldest) son.

---

[13] Frederick County Land Records, WR 7-123.

[14] Ibid., P-672.

[15] Ralph B. Strassburger and William J. Hinke, Pennsylvania German Pioneers (Norristown, Pa., 1934), vol. 1, p. 641, list 223C. On lists 223A and 223B he is carried as "Michael Kehner, on board," i.e., perhaps too sick to come ashore with the others.

He certainly was prepared to make a home for his family before 1754.

By a rather indefinite process of elimination, I assume that Jacob may have come to America considerably before 1750. Perhaps he even married here. Conversely, he may be the Jacob Koller who is listed as arriving in Philadelphia September 28, 1749 on the ship "Ann."[16] He may have had his family with him, since again only male adults were listed.

The early Lutheran Church marriage records identify two sons of Jacob Koller — Michael and Jacob.[17] The Church record lists also the birth on September 13, 1755 of a son, Johann Heinrich, to Jacob and his wife Magdalena.[18] If this is our Jacob Koller, as I strongly suspect, Johann Heinrich must have died in infancy, for there is apparently no record of him later than his baptism on October 31, 1755.

The Church record notes that on November 16, 1773 Jacob Koller, unmarried son of Jacob Koller, married Elisabeth Müllerin, unmarried daughter of Jacob Müller, "both living an der Huntin crick in Frederic county." On April 4, 1775 the record shows the marriage of Johannes Koller to Maria Müllerin, presumably also a daughter of Jacob Müller.[19] While this record doesn't identify John as Jacob's son, other evidence furnishes proof of that relationship.[20]

Jacob Müller was apparently a squatter, for I can find no record of land ownership by him. At any rate, he either moved elsewhere or had no estate at his death, for there is no will record or administration account to be found.

---

[16] Ibid., vol. 1, p. 417 (List #139C).
[17] Frederick Lutheran Church Book, loc. cit., pp. 261, 365 respectively.
[18] Ibid., p. 11.
[19] Ibid., p. 369.
[20] Frederick County Land Records, RP-177, WR 7-123. See below, pp. 116, 118.

There is also recorded on February 17, 1776 the birth of a daughter, Maria Magdalena, to Johannes Koller and his wife, Anna Maria. Complicating matters somewhat is the record on May 9, 1778 of the marriage of Johannes K̲eller to Maria Jostin, with Herman Jost and wife, Jacob K̲eller and wife, and Maria Müllerin as witnesses. For a considerable time I speculated that this was a second marriage for John Koller and that his first wife had died. I now think that, in spite of the interchangeable use of Keller and Koller in the Land Records, the parties to this 1778 marriage were Kellers and not Kollers.[21]

I doubt that the sequence of marriages of Michael, Jacob and John Koller, respectively 1772, 1773 and 1775, indicates the order of their ages. Michael was born in 1745; I estimate John's birth was in 1746/47 and Jacob's in 1748/49. I strongly suspect that John was the favorite son of Jacob The Elder, as certain events which I shall recite later seem to indicate.

As reference to the list of Jacob Koller's land transactions will indicate,[22] June 22, 1768 was a day of considerable importance. On that day were recorded deeds whereby he disposed of most of his holding of RAMSHORN, together with 200 acres of DEN OF WOLVES — some 860 acres in all. I think it is rather obvious that he was not living on RAMSHORN at that time — perhaps he had not lived on it since 1754.

Then, on August 18, 1777, he sold his final holding of DEN OF WOLVES. In view of the price he received for the 200 acres and the reservations he made in this final deed for his son John and for John Smith (who apparently was Michael's brother-in-law), it seems quite probable that these 200 acres contained

---

[21] Some substantiation comes from the Lutheran Church Book's consistently adhering in all other cases cited above to the Koller spelling as opposed to this single Keller reference. See also below, pp. 94-95.
[22] See again, pp. 114, 116, below.

his home dwelling. He may have lived on that part of
DEN OF WOLVES since 1762.

Obviously, also, Jacob was planning to retire
from farming, for slightly less than a month before
his last sale — on July 20, 1777 — he bought the west
half of Lot No. 136 in Frederick City for £40, subject
to a ground rent of £1 payable yearly to Daniel Dulany.[23] This half lot had a frontage on Third and Fourth
Streets of 30 feet and a depth of 393 feet. This depth
was the distance between Third and Fourth Streets,
and No. 136 was the third lot west of Middle Alley in
the first block of East Third and Fourth Streets.

Jacob must have used the proceeds of his land
sales to build a house on his Frederick lot, for on
June 5, 1780 he sold out to Jacob Baltzell, tailor, for
£2,000.[24] These transactions are listed in the records
as by Jacob Goller. Jacob's second wife, [Maria]
Magdalena, joined in the deed. The house was apparently destroyed, for on February 22, 1793 Baltzell,
then "of Allegany County," sold this half lot to Jacob
Fauble for £150.[25] The house at 27 East Third Street
now occupies this site.

Where did Jacob and Maria Magdalena go after
they sold their house in Frederick in 1780? There is
no definite answer to that question. But there is a
possible answer. On August 22, 1777 John Koller
(Hoeller, Cullers) bought 251 acres of land in
"Powell's Big Fort," Shenandoah County, Virginia.[26]
This transaction took place just four days after Jacob
Koller's last sale of DEN OF WOLVES, and I strongly
suspect that some of the proceeds of that sale may
have gone into this Virginia purchase.

This secluded part of Shenandoah County, lying

---

[23] Frederick County Land Records, RP-146.
[24] Ibid., WR 2-624.
[25] Ibid., WR 11-353.
[26] Shenandoah County Land Records, B-538. See
below, p. 126.

between two sharply rising mountains and between the North and South Branches of the Shenandoah River, was known variously as Powell's Big Fort, Powell's Fort and Fort Valley. It is a place to stir the imagination. Who, for instance, was William Powell who gave his name to this valley? I can find no historical <u>answer</u> to that. But there is a fictional answer. In John Esten Cooke's novel, <u>Fairfax; or the Master of Greenway Court</u>, copyrighted in 1868, Powell is painted as Sir William Powys, an impoverished English nobleman, who came to Virginia with his granddaughter hoping to recoup his fortunes.

Still according to the novel — and to current local legend — Powell found a silver mine in the mountains enclosing the valley, coined his own money therefrom, put into it more silver than similar legal coins contained and became the respected neighbor of Lord Fairfax of nearby Greenway Court. Cooke paints him as a man of distinguished bearing, living in a small cabin on the mountainside with his young granddaughter. For the benefit of any interested persons, I should add that Cooke also records in his novel that, since Powell was living on land then owned by Lord Fairfax, he dutifully laid aside a part of his silver as his Lordship's share, burying it in casks at various places in the mountains. Apparently these casks have never been found.

There is another fascinating half-legend, half-fact associated with this natural fortress-vally. It is historically true that George Washington, as a youth of sixteen, was surveying Fairfax's lands in that part of Virginia and doubtless knew Fort Valley well. It is said that General Washington, in the darkest hours of the Revolutionary War, had always in mind that if his armies suffered complete defeat elsewhere, he would retreat with their remnants to Powell's Fort Valley and there make a last stand. One or two historians hint at this, and Julia Davis in her excellent history of the Shenandoah Valley, gives it some credence.[27]

Imagine young John Koller of Frederick County

filling his saddle bags with cash on August 18, 1777 and dashing off through the wilderness to buy land in this almost inaccessible part of the Shenandoah Valley of Virginia, closing the deal four days later. How did he know about this strange place more than eighty miles from his Frederick County home? How, actually, did he find his way there? Certainly John, or more probably his father, had either some prior knowledge of the Valley or some close friend who knew about its fertile acres and perhaps guided John on his journey. It may even have been Jacob's "trusty friend, Lawrence Delauter," who sold his Middletown Valley land in 1773, although the first record I find of Delaughter's acquisition of land in Shenandoah County was on August 21, 1780, when he was granted 168 acres by Lord Fairfax,[28] He may, of course, have been a tenant or squatter before he acquired land.

Had Jacob himself been there earlier and moved into Maryland from Virginia in 1750? In the absence of definite information, this is almost pure speculation, of course. But there is some basis for such speculation. It is historically true, for instance, that some of the Germans who came early into the Carolinas and Virginia met various types of opposition there and to escape it moved northward as far as the Shenandoah Valley of Virginia. More specifically, there is the "History of the Culler Family" by Hugh Clayton Culler of Orangeburg, S. C., in which he states that in August 1735 one Benedict Koller arrived in Charleston, S. C., and became the "founder of the Culler Family in the Carolinas and Georgia."[29] Ob-

---

[27] Julia Davis, The Shenandoah, Rivers of America Series (New York, 1945), pp. 11, 331.

[28] Shenandoah County Land Records, N-2.

[29] I have not seen Hugh Culler's History. The foregoing was taken from Mr. Aaron A. Culler's "Information about Some Culler Families" (1938). Mr. Aaron Culler is now deceased and his monograph,

viously, therefore, there were Kollers among the early Germans coming into the Carolinas and Jacob could quite possibly have been one of them, joining the migration northward to Virginia.

I find nothing in the records to indicate when John actually moved to Powell's Fort. In view of the provisions for him in the deed of 1777 to Shriver, John may have remained in Maryland until 1778. I think there is no doubt that by 1780, when his father sold his house in Frederick City, John was established in Fort Valley, and I suspect Jacob and Maria Magdalena went to live with them, for there is no further evidence of land purchase by them in Frederick County, Maryland. Jacob still owned Lot No. 13 in Myer's Addition to Frederick, which he transferred to John in 1787. John sold this lot to Martin Keplinger on March 20, 1789 for £17.[30] Because Maria Magdalena hadn't joined in the deed to John, it was necessary for her to join John's deed to Keplinger. She was obviously, therefore, still living in March of 1789.

John died in 1796, some time between September 16 and December 13, when his will was probated.[31] But Jacob survived his son. In this will John, now known as John Cullers, provides that his wife Mary shall have all his property until the youngest child shall reach twenty-one (or she remarries), after which the "land and other property that remains after schooling my children and the expenses of supporting and keeping my father who at present is living with me," shall be sold by his executors and divided equally between his children. He names his wife and Henry Burner, a son-in-law, executors, but unfortunately doesn't list his childrens' names. Henry Burner had

---

dealing primarily with Michael Culler and his descendants in Ohio, was loaned me by Mrs. David R. Culler, R.D. #1, Lucas, Ohio.

[30] Frederick County Land Records, WR 8-393.

[31] Shenandoah County Will Records, 3-58.

married Magdalena Cullers before her 18th birthday by a license dated November 9, 1793.[32]

Under date of December 26, 1812, Jacob Danner and his wife Cathy (Cullers) with Jacob Cullers and his wife Betsy (Ridenour), all of Hardy County, [West] Virginia, deeded to their mother all their interest in John's lands.[33] On March 17, 1816 Mary Cullers and Henry Burner, executors, deeded to Henry Cullers (obviously John's son) for $750 John's lands in Powell's Big Fort "on both sides of Passage Creek [which flows through Fort Valley]....part of 251 acres conveyed to John Cullers August 22, 1777 by John Conrad Teboe and Esther."[34]

On my summary of Jacob Koller's sales of RAMS-HORN[35] I have placed the words "his mother" after the word "widow" on the deed of June 22, 1768 to Eliza-beth Keller. Jacob didn't call her his mother; in his deed he merely designated her as "widow." But Eliza-beth called him "her son" in a deed of October 23, 1773.[36] Some time between 1768 and 1773 Elizabeth married one Andrew Smith, about whom I know only that he apparently lived in the vicinity of RAMSHORN. In this 1773 deed she and Andrew were selling to John Keller (Koller) for £260 the 100 acres of RAMSHORN conveyed to Elizabeth "by her son, Jacob Keller, on or about June 22, 1768."

Actually, I doubt that Elizabeth was Jacob's mother. I think she was his step-mother. Any son with a normal amount of filial love and respect would describe his widowed mother as something more than "widow," particularly when, on the same day, in another deed, he described Andrew Keller as his broth-er and indicates his desire to provide for his welfare.

---

[32] Shenandoah County Marriage Records.
[33] Shenandoah County Land Records, U-111.
[34] Ibid., W-391.
[35] See below, p. 114.
[36] Frederick County Land Records, U-178.

Moreover, by a combination of geriatrics and simple arithmetic, it seems almost impossible. Assume, as I believe, that Michael, born in 1745, was Jacob's oldest son. Few men of that day became legitimate fathers before they were at least 21 years old — and the average age was probably nearer 25. About the earliest age at which Elizabeth could have become Jacob's mother was 16. Sixteen plus 21 equals 37. Elizabeth, therefore, would scarcely have been less than 37 in 1745. That would put her birth date at 1708. But she was still living in November 1804, when her husband, Andrew Smith, made his will.[37] She would therefore in 1804 have been a minimum of 96 years old — not impossible, but highly improbable.

There is one more interesting bit of information in Andrew Smith's will. He speaks of owing "my stepson Andrew Keller twenty pounds" and directs his executor to pay the debt.

All this speculation about Jacob and Elizabeth raises new questions. Who was Jacob's father? Did he die in America? If he died in Europe, why and when did his widow come to America? I leave it to others to find the answers, but invite their attention to my further notes on pages 111-113, below.

Up to this point I have not indicated any of the doubts which long plagued me as to whether Jacob Keller of RAMSHORN was also the Jacob Keller of DEN OF WOLVES. By church and land records it was not too difficult to prove that the latter was actually Jacob Koller (Culler). For the benefit of some interested Culler descendant who, I hope, may some day take up the Culler story where I leave it, I think I should list some of the causes of these doubts and some of the clues which resolved them in my own mind sufficiently to cause me to feel justified in presenting my material in its present form.

In these earlier days when one encounters two or

---

[37] Frederick County Wills, GMRB 1-369.

more individuals with the same name, it is difficult to follow any specific one of them. There are, however, two principal clues: wives' names and descriptions of land owned. In the current effort, for instance, I have had considerable difficulty in separating Jacob The Elder from several Jacob Kellers, and even from his son and grandsons, also Jacobs and also frequently found in the records as Kellers. Sometimes the chief clue was a wife's name signed to a deed.

One Jacob Keller died intestate in 1765 and hence was quite definitely a contemporary and possible owner of RAMSHORN (See pages 111-113: I think he was quite probably Jacob Koller "The Eldest," the father of Jacob "The Elder.") His administrators were Elizabeth and Jacob Keller, their relationship to him unknown, although the surviving Jacob Keller could have been a son. A Jacob Keller, whom I shall discuss later, died in 1824 owning approximately 150 acres of RAMSHORN land. Could the Jacob Keller who died in 1765 have been the 1750 purchaser of the 102 acres of RAMSHORN from Rhodes and have obtained the 1765 resurvey of 812 acres on RAMSHORN? I do not think so. (1) The inventory of his estate consisted entirely of personal property. (2) He could not have executed the five deeds recorded in June of 1768. (3) If he had owned RAMSHORN and by some obscure unknown process the Jacob who survived him came into possession of it and he executed the 1768 deeds, he would have been obliged for purposes of title clarity to indicate in these deeds the basis of his ownership. There is no such indication in any of them beyond the statement that the tract conveyed is part of the RESURVEY ON RAMSHORN "obtained by Jacob Keller."

Could this Jacob Keller (died 1824) have been the son of the Jacob Keller (died 1765) and himself the original purchaser of RAMSHORN in 1750? If so, he would have had to be a minimum of 21 years of age in 1750 and hence born not later than 1729. The only Jacob Keller who is known to have owned any part of RAMSHORN after 1768 was the Jacob mentioned above who died in 1824, but whose parentage is unknown. He would therefore have been at least 95 years old at his death, and I apply the same skepticism to him that I applied to the "mother" of Jacob The Elder.

But there are complications which raise some embarrassing questions. Dr. Grace L. Tracey very kindly platted for me the five deeds of June 1768, superimposed on the original RAMSHORN and RESURVEY ON RAMSHORN (see page 115). This platting indicates that 102 acres of RAMSHORN (the original 1750 purchase from Rhodes) was not transferred! Yet Jacob Keller (died 1824) owned it at his death — divided, however, into two tracts of $91\frac{1}{4}$ acres and $10\frac{3}{4}$ acres! That certainly seems to indicate that he had been the original purchaser in 1750 and had obtained the resurvey in 1765, retaining the original purchase until his death. I do not believe this is true, but feel there are somewhere one or more unrecorded deeds transferring ownership perhaps back and forth between Kellers and Kollers.

Waive, for the present, my skepticism about this Jacob Keller's age. Consider him, therefore, the brother of Andrew Keller and the son of Elizabeth Keller. We then observe the following transactions: In 1768 he gave Andrew 100 acres of his RESURVEY ON RAMSHORN to help him get started in life. On September 17, 1792 Andrew sold these 100 acres back to Jacob for £300[38] — a rather substantial profit at his "brother's" expense, especially since Jacob didn't intend to keep these 100 acres.

Less than eight months later Jacob sold it to Frederick Stemple for £300. This sale took place in a reciprocal transaction on May 2, 1793, wherein Stemple deeded Jacob Keller for £500 150 acres of RESURVEY ON RAMSHORN.[39] This was part of the 250 acres Stemple had bought from John Keller (Koller) for

---

[38] Frederick County Land Records, WR 11-91.
[39] Ibid., WR 11-546.

£400 on March 10, 1789.[40] (John had bought 150 acres of this from Jacob The Elder for £10 in June 1768 and 100 acres from Elizabeth Keller Smith for £260 in 1773.) Jacob and Ann Mary then deeded back to Stemple for £800 250 acres of the RESURVEY ON RAMS-HORN,[41] being the 150 acres from Stemple and the 100 acres they had bought from Andrew and Charlotte in 1792.

In spite of these profitless sales of land he once owned (still assuming he _was_ the original owner), parts or all of which he could have retained from the beginning, Jacob seemed anxious to own more of RAMSHORN. On March 12, 1798 he paid Jacob Nye £100 for 22 acres.[42] And, strangely enough, these 22 acres were part of the 250 acres Stemple had bought from John Keller (Koller) in 1789. Stemple sold the 22 acres for £60 to Henry Bletcher[43] on the very same day, May 2, 1793, on which he had the simultaneous transaction with Jacob Keller. The 22 acres had passed through the hands of four owners between 1793 and 1798: Bletcher, Booker, Haupt and Nye.

This series of transactions is scarcely what one would expect the original owner of the entire tract to make. If he so strongly desired RAMSHORN land, the easiest way to have it would have been to keep it in the first place — not dispose of it wholesale in 1768 and then buy it back in small retail lots later.

Jacob Keller's will was made October 2, 1822 and probated January 3, 1825. In it he states that his two sons, Jacob and David, have farmed his land for him for the past 15 years, but that David is about to leave him, so that he gives the land to Jacob. David is given $200, payable by his brother Jacob. He also mentions that his son Abraham is deceased.

---

[40]   Ibid., WR 8-377.
[41]   Ibid., WR 11-581.
[42]   Ibid., WR 16-291.
[43]   Ibid., WR 11-598.

On August 25, 1827 Jacob, Jr., bought $21\frac{3}{4}$ acres of RESURVEY ON RAMSHORN from Frederick Stemple for $831.25, or $38 per acre.[44] If, therefore, the Jacob Keller (Sr.) who died in 1824 had been the owner of the original 812 acres of RESURVEY ON RAMSHORN, it is something of an anomaly to find his son buying part of it back, especially at a rather substantial per-acre price.

Then in 1833 Jacob, Jr., applied to the Land Office for a resurvey of all his lands. There were five parcels, the source of only two of which is evident in the land records. I think he was doubtful about the clarity of title to some of his RAMSHORN holdings. For instance, the deed to the 22 acres his father bought in 1798 remained in the Court House until March 2, 1826, when Jacob picked it up more than a year after his father's death and 28 years after its execution. When he couldn't find record of other deeds to RAMSHORN land, he apparently decided to ask the State for a resurvey and a patent. This resurvey was called PLEASANT RETREAT,[45] but there is no record in the Maryland Land Office that a patent based on this resurvey was ever issued.

In view of all the foregoing, I can only conclude that Jacob Keller (d. 1824) was not the original owner of RAMSHORN and RESURVEY ON RAMSHORN and that Jacob Koller The Elder was himself that original owner.

Incidentally, the Kellers belonged to the Reformed Church and the Kollers were Lutherans. And I find in the records under date of April 5, 1791 an agreement between the trustees of the Reformed and Lutheran Churches in Middletown, Maryland, to which one Jacob Keller is one of the signatories for the Reformed Church and Michael Coller (Koller) a signer for the Lutheran Church.[46] (I know of no other Jacob Keller

---

[44] Ibid., JS 28-154.
[45] Frederick County Survey Records, THO 1-481.

94

the Middletown community who at that time was of an age and such standing in his community as the Jacob Keller who died in 1824.)

There was also similar confusion between the two John Keller (Koller) marriages mentioned earlier.[47] Both appeared in the Frederick Lutheran Church Book: A Johannes Keller (surname so spelled in the record) married Maria Müller on April 4, 1775, but a Johannes Keller married Maria Jost on May 9, 1778. Were they the same man, and if not which was a Koller and which got part of RAMSHORN in 1768?

One of the June 22, 1768 deeds issued by Jacob Keller (who I believe to be actually Jacob Koller The Elder) was to a John Keller for 150 acres of RESUR-VEY ON RAMSHORN, the consideration being £10. That price was much below that charged the others on the same day — except, of course, his young half[?]-brother Andrew. Since Jacob had a son John, it seemed obvious that this concession was to a son.

A John Keller and his wife Ann M. were buried in the Frederick Lutheran Cemetery.[48] According to the gravestone, he died on March 18, 1831, aged 78. Hence he was born in 1753. His wife died on March 22, 1848, aged 86, and was therefore born in 1762. It seems rather logical to assume that this was not the couple married in 1775, for he would then have been 22 and she only 13. Instead, they were undoubtedly the John Keller and Mary Jost who were married in 1778.

That John Keller, however, couldn't have become the owner of part of RAMSHORN in 1768, since he would then have been only 15 years old. Since there is no other John Keller known to me sufficiently con-temporary to this period, I conclude that John Keller

[46] Frederick County Land Records, WR 10-25.
[47] See above, pp. 83-84.
[48] Jacob Mehrling Holdcraft, Names In Stone (Ann Arbor, Michigan, 1966), vol. 1, p. 645.

of the 1768 deed was actually John Koller, son of Jacob Koller The Elder, that he married [Anna] Maria [Magdalena] Müller in 1775 and that he was later known as John Cullers of Virginia.

Two deeds, considered together, seem to me to be strong confirmation of this conclusion. In one, dated March 10, 1789, John Keller and his wife "Modelona" of "Frederick County, Maryland" conveyed to Frederick Stemple 250 acres of RAMSHORN.[49] Consider this deed now in connection with one dated just 10 days later, March 20, 1789, and indexed "Maria Culler, et al., "transferring Lot No. 13 in Myers Addition to Frederick City to Martin Keplinger for £17.[50] The wording of this deed taken in conjunction with the John Keller deed to Stemple reveals a great deal by its confusions and omissions.

I quote its salient parts: "Between <u>Maria</u> Culler, wife of John [the lawyer who wrote this meant Jacob, as is evident below] Culler, late of Frederick County, Maryland, but now of Shenandoah County, Virginia, and John Culler, son and assignee of the <u>said</u> Jacob Culler of the state and county first mentioned, farmer, and Martin Keplinger, of the county and state last mentioned, weaver [study that and tell me, please, who lived where!]....Witnesseth that the <u>said Magdalena</u> Culler and John Culler....have....sold....Lot No. 13 (40 x 339 feet on the South Side of the road or street)...." Magdalena and John both signed — but not by mark.

Appended to this deed was the customary acknowledgement: "Then came Magdalena Culler and John Culler....and at the same time came Mary Culler, wife of John Culler...." who released her right of dower.

In spite of all this confusion of names and places of residence by some befuddled lawyer, I think the

---

[49] Frederick County Land Records, WR 8-377.
[50] Ibid., WR 8-393. Cf. Jacob's 1787 deed to his son John, ibid., WR 7-123.

picture is quite clear. John and Mary wanted to sell their Maryland land holdings. Since Magdalena hadn't released her dower right when her husband deeded Lot No. 13 to his son in 1787, in order to give clear title to that parcel, it was necessary for her to sign the deed transferring it.

For reasons known only to themselves, John and Mary decided to travel to Frederick County to effect the sales and execute the deeds, and obviously Maria Magdalena was obliged to accompany them. Perhaps Jacob came too, and the four visited relatives while the sales were being consummated.

There are two other questions: (1) Why were John and Mary described as "of Frederick County, Maryland"? The answer, I think, is very simple. They were present in Maryland, prepared to execute deeds to Maryland properties. Why cloud the issue by showing their residence elsewhere? (2) And why not use the name as they were now calling themselves — Cullers? John had acquired the RAMSHORN land as John Keller, it being shown thus in all the records. A clear and unbroken chain of title made the continued use of Keller preferable in this transaction.

I was never able to solve the riddle of Jacob's half[?]-brother Andrew. His wife's name was Charlotte, spelled generally "Sharlot" in the records, followed him to Frederick County, Virginia in 1799 and in Frederick County, Maryland to 1824, when he sold the last of his land holdings and disappeared. He remained Keller to the end in all the records. Charlotte had apparently died in 1823, and it is quite probable that Andrew went to Virginia after selling out in Maryland. If I ever have opportunity to search the Virginia records more thoroughly, I may well find him there as Andrew Cullers!

A final word about the confusion of Kollers and Kellers, out of which arose the question whether Jacob Keller (so spelled in the deed records) of RAMSHORN was the Jacob Keller (also so spelled in the deed records) of DEN OF WOLVES, the latter without doubt being actually Jacob Koller The Elder:

In an effort to prove or disprove a connection between the Kellers and Kollers, Mr. John P. Dern compiled for me, from many sources, an exhaustive list of dozens of names — some spelled Koller, but most spelled Keller — showing whatever information and family relationships were available to him.

Using this list as a basis, I have examined dozens of Frederick County deeds, wills and estate accounts. I can identify as Kollers (Cullers) all his names so spelled. His Kellers fall roughly into three geographical groups: (1) Those in the area east of Frederick City; (2) Those northeast of Frederick, on Monocacy Manor and along the Monocacy River; and (3) Those in the Middletown-Myersville area, none of whom was apparently contemporary with the early ownership of RAMSHORN. Some members of each of these groups became Frederick City residents.

I can find no family connection between these Kellers and Kollers. And the earliest record of land ownership by anyone definitely a Keller in the Middletown-Myersville area is March 18, 1767, when two Keller brothers, Abraham and Philip (ancestry unknown) bought identical acreages for identical considerations from Christian KEMP.[51] The land they bought apparently lay east-northeast of Middletown.

A most striking differentiation between the Kellers and Kollers was their church membership. I cannot find a single Koller who wasn't a Lutheran; and with only a few rare exceptions the Kellers were members of the German Reformed Church.

All of this convinces me that the Kellers were Kellers, that the Keller-Kollers were Kollers and that never do the twain meet!

In spite of all the contrary possibilities which I have been discussing, there is one piece of evidence which most strongly influences my belief that Jacob

---

[51] Ibid., K-1065, K-1070.

Keller of RAMSHORN and Jacob Keller of DEN OF
WOLVES are one and the same. That evidence is the
recording of seven deeds on June 22, 1768 by a Jacob
Keller whose wife's name was Mary. Five of these
concerned RAMSHORN and two DEN OF WOLVES. It
scarcely seems within the probabilities of coincidence
that a Jacob and Mary Keller would execute five deeds
to RAMSHORN, while another and different Jacob and
Mary Keller (whom I know to be Kollers) were on the
same day executing two deeds to DEN OF WOLVES.

In my opinion, also, the Kellers (Kollers) of
RAMSHORN and DEN OF WOLVES are tied together
by the notations made by the Clerk of the Court indi-
cating delivery of the four deeds of John, Andrew,
Elizabeth and Michael. Michael, who I know was
Michael Koller (Culler) and who received 100 acres of
DEN OF WOLVES, was delivered the deed of his
brother John who got 150 acres of RAMSHORN.[52]

Thus far I have been treating the Koller family
primarily as a family, and what I have set down about
its several members and their contemporaries has
been designed to show, as best I could, the broad
family connections and movements. As I said at the
outset, it had not been my intention to write a complete history of the Culler family. What follows,
therefore, while it deals specifically with Jacob's
three sons, John, Jacob and Michael, is intended to
record, for whatever value and interest it may have,
what I have learned about these sons and have not previously mentioned. In the case of Michael, since I
descend from him through my mother and know more
about him, I shall go into somewhat more detail.

I have included on page 119 a family chart to the
third generation from Jacob the Elder, which is ac-

------

[52] See below, pp 114-115.

curate (except where otherwise noted in the text) according to my present knowledge. It is, of course, subject to revision on the basis of future findings.

JOHN

John, who bought land in Virginia in 1777, had eight children, and his descendants through the male line spell their family name with an added "s" — Cullers. Lt. Col. Lewis E. Martin, retired, of Radcliff, Kentucky, a Cullers descendant, has written a voluminous history of this branch of the family. I have not seen this work, but Col. Martin writes me that it is in nine volumes and contains 2488 pages. He has sent me copies of six prefatory pages of his history. I have no desire to be critical of the work of another family historian, realizing my own vulnerability, but he has obviously drawn upon the same inaccurate and confused sources which others have used and which it has been my primary purpose to correct.

In his preface, Col. Martin says: "It cannot be stated as a positive and provable fact that John Cullers who bought land in Shenandoah County, Virginia, is the same John Cullers who lived in Frederick County, Maryland." I like to think that I have finally proved that fact in the foregoing text, and reference is again made to the 1777 deed on page 126.

I am indebted to Col. Martin and also to Mr. Orie Munch, of Seven Fountains, Virginia, for the names of John's children. (See chart, page 119.) Mr. Munch, a Cullers descendant, owns eighty acres of the original John Culler farm.

Of passing interest, perhaps, is the fact that Catherine Cullers married Jacob Danner, and, as noted above (page 89), they were in Hardy County, [West] Virginia in 1812. I suspect that Jacob may have been the son of one Jacob Danner of Shenandoah County who achieved some reputation as a clockmaker and who once owned more than 800 acres of SPRING PLAINS in Frederick County, Maryland.

Here, for whatever value it may have, perhaps I should interject a quotation from Mr. Munch's letter of December 1967. Speaking of John, he writes, "It was during a visit to his sister, wife of one John Bushong, at their plantation....in Powell's Fort Valley, that he found an adjoining plantation for sale." This is the only mention I have ever encountered of a daughter of Jacob The Elder.

I have not had the opportunity to try to verify this through Virginia land records, or otherwise. If true, it would have a triple effect: (1) It would explain why John bought land so far away from his Maryland home; (2) it would strengthen the theory of Jacob's migration northward into Maryland; and (3) in line with the foregoing, it would be at least partial explanation for Jacob's retirement to Virginia with John rather than his remaining in Maryland with his other two sons: he was perhaps going back to old and familiar surroundings.

JACOB

Of the Elder Jacob's three sons, I have been able to learn less about Jacob than about the other two. So far as I know, Jacob II, unlike his brothers, never acquired land from his father. Whether this fact has any significance I do not know. I strongly suspect that the principal reason for this may have been his age. I estimate his birth to have occurred about 1748/49, and if this is correct, he was under legal age in 1768 when his father disposed of most of his lands. His first purchase of land in Frederick County was in 1780, when he bought 100 acres of RESURVEY ON GRIND-STONE ROCK from Daniel Bussard.[53]

In this 1780 deed, Jacob is described as a weaver, as was John Smith, Michael's brother-in-law, in his 1778 deed selling his 100 acres of DEN OF WOLVES.[54]

---

[53] Frederick County Land Records, WR 2-468.
[54] Ibid., RP-464.

I think it is highly probable that Jacob Koller and John Smith were employed in the Wickham weaving mills near the mouth of Hunting Creek, probably along what is now Shryock Road. In the estate account of Samuel Wickham, who was apparently a weaving mill operator, under date of February 1776, is an item, "Paid Jacob Coller on note, 2 pounds, 16 shillings."[55]

I do not know where "an der Huntin crick" Jacob and Elizabeth lived from the time of their marriage in 1773 until 1780. He sold his GRINDSTONE ROCK land in 1795,[56] and again his place of abode is unknown to me until 1802 when he bought from John and Catherine Culler — who I suspect were his son and daughter-in-law — Lots 36, 37 and part of 38 in the town of Woodsboro.[57] He evidently lived on Lot 38, for when he sold these lots in 1810, the land description read, "Beginning at the northwest corner of Lot 38, which is the northwest corner of Jacob Culler's dwelling house on said lot...."[58]

Jacob II was first described as "Senior" in an 1807 deed,[59] definitely indicating that his father was dead. Jacob's son, Jacob III, who then became "Junior," had married Mary Storm, daughter of one Michael Sturm, in 1795 when he had just passed his twentieth birthday. They probably lived with either Mary's parents or his own until he acquired about 60 acres from Jacob, Sr., in 1808.[60]

Meanwhile, Jacob Sr., had bought from the four surviving Storm heirs all their interests in their father's land. Jacob Storm, a son, executed his deed in Sullivan County, Tennessee,[61] and Michael Storm,

---

55 Frederick County Administrative Accounts, G M 1-7.
56 Frederick County Land Records, WR 13-119/120.
57 Ibid., WR 23-59.
58 Ibid., WR 37-655.
59 Ibid., WR 30-412.
60 Ibid., WR 33-122.
61 Ibid., WR 30-412.

another son, did so in Fairfield County, Ohio.[62] The 60 acres deeded Jacob, Jr., in 1808, were part of the Storm lands. Jacob, Sr., disposed of the last of his landholdings on September 15, 1815[63] and disappears from the records. Jacob, Jr., had sold his 60 acres to Philip Culler (quite probably his brother) on September 17, 1811,[64] after which he also disappears. I have no present idea where either went.

My family chart on page 119 shows seven children for Jacob II. Three of these are confirmed, with their birth dates, by the early Frederick Lutheran Church Book. The last three I find in the 1934 Zahn translation of the Middletown Lutheran Church Book.[65] I have merely interpolated the birth year shown for son John, and hence I cannot guarantee its accuracy.

As noted previously, I think the John Culler who sold Jacob II the Woodsboro lots was quite probably Jacob's son. One of the strongest arguments for this is the fact that I know of no other John Culler who fits into the pattern. Then there is that four-year interval between the births of Jacob and Catherine. What would be more logical, therefore, than a son John born in 1777, a son old enough to marry Catherine Groshon in 1799? John and Catherine disappear from the records after their sale of the Woodsboro lots in 1802.

On May 25, 1805 one Nathaniel Woodward married a Mary Culler.[66] I cannot identify either of them.

---

[62] Ibid., WR 32-14.
[63] Ibid., JS 1-470.
[64] Ibid., WR 40-408.
[65] "Church Record of the Lutheran Congregation of Zion Church at Middletown, near Frederick, Md.," translated by Charles T. Zahn (Typescript, Westminster, Md., December 1934).
[66] Frederick County Marriage Licenses. Mary, daughter of John Culler, was married in Virginia in 1801.

However, one Philip Culler, who I suspect was the son of Jacob II, in March 1812 had a real estate transaction with Nathaniel Woodward.[67] On April 3, 1812 Philip Culler sold for $1,280 the approximately 60 acres he had acquired from Jacob III in September 1811.[68] No wife is shown in Philip's real estate transactions, and he disappears from the records thereafter.

One Catherine Coller married Jacob Baker in April 1810.[69] While this might be the daughter of Jacob II, it seems to me rather doubtful. Since Jacob's Catherine was born in 1779, she would have been 31 years old in 1810 — a very late age for marriage in those early days. But if this is not Jacob's Catherine, then I do not know what became of her. Nor do I know anything further about Catherine Coller Baker, although there is one other possibility: Since John Culler's wife was named Catherine and since he disappears from the records after 1802, Catherine Coller Baker might possibly be John's widow.

There is another Jacob Culler who perhaps should be mentioned here, although I cannot now connect him with any of the other Cullers. I cannot find his marriage in the Frederick County Marriage Records. But he was married to Magdalena Rusher probably before 1802, for in that year the Clerk of the Court delivered to him, on order of John Rusher, Magdalena's father, an 1800 deed of Rusher's. John Rusher died intestate sometime between 1802 and 1806, for on February 14, 1806 Jacob and Magdalena deeded to Godfrey Leatherman Magdalena's 1/6th interest in certain of her father's lands.[70] They executed a similar deed on September 13, 1815 to Dennis Hanley, conveying her interest in her father's interest in FOUNTAIN LOW.[71]

---

[67] Frederick County Land Records, WR 41-647.
[68] Ibid., WR 42-58.
[69] Frederick County Marriage Records.
[70] Frederick County Land Records, WR 28-290.
[71] Ibid., JS 3-498.

The deed of December 8, 1800 from Conrad Lich-lider to John Rusher, conveying part of GREEN SPRING and part of FIRST DIVIDEND, refers in its courses and distances as extending "to Michael Coller's land."[72] These tracts were in the DEN OF WOLVES area, but since Michael Culler had sold his holdings there in 1774, I cannot understand the reference thereto 26 years later.

At least two family historians mention the marriage of a Jacob Culler to a Magdalena Busch. I quote one[73] of them: "One son [of Michael], Jacob Culler, born in 1782, with Magdalena Busch, eloped from the home of[sic] Koon's Ridge, Warren Township, Franklin County, Pennsylvania, where they built a humble home in the woods...." I mention this Jacob (1) because of the possible confusion of the names Busch and Rusher, and (2) to correct any impression that the Jacob who eloped "was the son of Michael, son of Jacob The Elder.

MICHAEL

Early in this account I devoted considerable time and space to establishing — I hope for all time — the name of Michael Culler's wife. I did this because there seemed to be so much confusion about her name among those members of the family who have written about it.

There is an equal confusion on the part of at least some of these writers — and, indeed, most members of the family — about the early Koller immigrants. For instance, in the History of Frederick County, previously referred to,[74] my Uncle Millard Culler repeats the legend so present and so popular among so many families, about the three brothers who came to

---

[72] Ibid., WR 20-526.
[73] See above, p. 87, note 29.
[74] Williams and McKinsey, op. cit., p. 1085.

America and settled respectively in Pennsylvania, Maryland and Virginia. With all due respect to my dear and favorite uncle and namesake, I am obliged to say that, so far as the Kollers are concerned, he was grossly in error. Jacob The Elder, of course, had three sons, but Uncle Millard wasn't talking about them, and I doubt that he knew about them. And they all grew up in Maryland with their father and mother.

Another thing the family historians — or at least most of them — keep repeating is that Michael first bought land in Middletown Valley in 1763. In view of Michael's birth in 1745, the statement must be false on its face. He would have been only 18 years old in 1763 and hence legally unable to hold title to land. He bought 100 acres of DEN OF WOLVES from his father in 1768 and sold it in 1774 to Henry Lenhart for £175.[75]

Incidentally, Michael's land lay in the southwest part of DEN OF WOLVES, very close to present-day Lewistown, and it is quite possible that a part of that town lies on it. The exactness of this statement is clouded by a resurvey on this tract (or a part of it) obtained by John Cronise in 1798, resulting in a 207-acre tract renamed ELDEST SON.[76]

The first deed to Michael for land in Middletown Valley which I can find was recorded on August 21, 1776, when Conrad Ricker conveyed 100 acres, part of MATTHEWS GOOD WILL, to Michael for £250.[77] I offer a first-class steak dinner to the first person who can find for me an earlier deed to Michael for Middletown Valley land.

Then there is the matter of the confiscation of Michael's property. There are two versions. One has it that Michael was an ardent patriot and because of that his property was confiscated by the British. I have consulted a number of knowledgeable Maryland

---

[75] Frederick County Land Records, V-347.
[76] Frederick County Patented Certificate #1250.
[77] Frederick County Land Records, BD2-338.

106

historians, and they assure me they have never heard of any confiscation by the British of property in Frederick County — and, incidentally, neither have I.

The other version has it that Michael was a Tory and his property was confiscated by the State of Maryland in 1781 when the state seized and sold Tory property within the state. I'm sure the DAR and those of Michael's descendants who joined that organization on the basis of his loyalty would find that version slightly embarrassing. For the benefit of any descendants desiring to join either the DAR or SAR, Michael Coller is shown to have served on the Committee of Observation for the Middle District of Frederick County between September 12, 1775 and October 24, 1776. [78]

So far as I know, Michael is the ancestor of all the Cullers in Maryland and of those in Ohio who spell their name without the final "s." Obviously there are many descendants scattered elsewhere. Some of the family historians list nine children for Michael and Eleanor, adding one named Lenora for her mother. If there ever was a daughter Lenora, she didn't live to maturity. There is also a family tradition that a son died at twelve years of age of typhoid fever.

In any event, only eight children reached maturity. These I have listed below, with their birth, marriage and death dates and their places of burial. [79] These same eight children are listed in Michael's will. [80] Because I descend through Michael's son Henry, who was my great grandfather, I include herein similar information relative to his family and also that of my grandfather Daniel. [81]

The places of burial shown on the first of these lists indicate that three of Michael's sons, Jacob, Philip and Michael, migrated to Ohio. This emigra-

---

[78] Maryland Historical Magazine, vol. 11, p. 164.
[79] See pp. 120-121.
[80] Frederick County Will Records, HS 2-145.
[81] See below, pp. 122-123.

tion took place about 1825, and some of their descendants in Ohio say that one of the strongest influences on their westward move was their opposition to slavery.

It was once stated that the Culler Family is of Scotch ancestry.[82] In view of the name — Koller — that statement is almost absurd. Koller is as German as sauerkraut. And down through the generations the Kollers-Cullers seem to have intermarried primarily with persons of German descent. My own mother and father are one of the few exceptions of which I am aware. The Rices are of English origin.

Speaking of Germans: The early German immigrants into Frederick County found no warm welcome. The wealthy and aristocratic English land speculators, who preceded them, exploited them. Their tax collectors victimized them to such a degree that many moved away — many to the Shenandoah Valley of Virginia. And those who remained petitioned for redress. Most of the land they acquired they bought, and those who received grants were awarded relatively small tracts — generally in the less desirable sections of the County.

This brings me back to Jacob Koller The Elder. I think he must have been a man of considerable ability and ambition. I know of no other German who acquired so much land without buying it. He bought and paid for 202 acres, but by means of resurveys he acquired 1,387 additional acres, making a total of 1,589. While some 274 acres of this was apparently later found to be foul of older surveys, the 1,315 acres which he sold made a very impressive total for a German.

The "drive" shown by Jacob reappeared in some of his descendants. Captain Henry, for instance, is known by the family as a "hard-boiled" entrepreneur. Tradition has it that at one time he owned so much land that he could travel from Jefferson to Frederick with-

---

[82] Williams and McKinsey, op. cit., p. 1027.

out getting off his own property. He was one of the incorporators of the Frederick and Harper's Ferry Turnpike and of the Jefferson Savings Institution formed in 1832. And he had a chain of three or more stores in Jefferson, Upperville in Virginia and Shepherdstown in West Virginia.

Then there was Capt. Henry's son, Col. Henry, who wasn't a Colonel at all, except by courtesy of being appointed to the Governor's Staff in return for political activity and contributions. He had inherited and married wealth. He died when I was seven years old, and I vaguely remember a large and imperious old man with a heavy cane and, still more vaguely, the whisperings about some of his crusty behavior. In contrast, however, to these two Henrys was Captain Henry's grandson, my Uncle Millard Culler, who was one of the kindest and gentlest of men.

Somewhat apologetically I present the foregoing brief epilogue about some Culler characteristics for whatever value and interest it may have.

MEMBERSHIP ELIGIBILITY
IN PATRIOTIC SOCIETIES

Because I happen to have it, I append the following for the benefit of any Culler descendants who may desire membership in certain of the patriotic societies. I have already referred to Michael's service. [83]

Those who descend from Capt. Henry are perhaps eligible for membership in the Society of the War of 1812 by reason of his service therein. They may possibly be additionally eligible for membership in the Revolutionary War societies through Henry's wife, Anna Feaster, since her grandfather, Henry Feaster, was a Captain in the German Battalion. However, there is apparently some cloud on Capt. Feaster's military record which may indicate either disloyalty or incompetence. His record as supplied by the National Archives in Washington, D. C., reads: "Cashiered, April 7, 1777," and the record ends at that point. For a period thereafter the Company he commanded is listed as "vacant."

Those who descend from Capt. Henry's son Daniel are additionally eligible for the Revolutionary Societies through Daniel's wife Ann Maria Hargett, whose grandfather Abraham Hargett (Hargis) was a Lieutenant in the 10th Pennsylvania Regiment. [84]

---

[83] See above, p. 107.
[84] Pennsylvania Archives, Fifth Series, vol. 2, pp. 434, 439, 442; vol. 3, pp. 471, 479, 494.

JACOB KOLLER THE ELDEST?

I am now about to set down a bit of genealogical circumstantial evidence which may be completely valueless, but which I find mightily intriguing. It concerns the possible father of Jacob The Elder and hence the husband of Elizabeth, Jacob's 'mother."

Remembering that for a long time the Kollers were listed in all the public records as Kellers, I began to cast about for a Keller who died about 1767/68 and might, therefore, have been the husband of Elizabeth. In the records of administrators' accounts in the Orphans Court of Frederick County I found the first and final account of the estate of one Jacob Keller late of Frederick County," dated May 17, 1770.[85] And who do you suppose were the administrators? Why, Elizabeth and Jacob Keller!

The Inventory for the estate "of Jacob Keller of Frederick County, lately deceased" was made November 25, 1765 by Samuel Buzard and Henry Fister (Feaster). It was customary at that time for one or more creditors of the deceased to approve an inventory and for one or more close relatives of the deceased to co-sign. This inventory bears the notation: "Creditors: there is none; Kinn, Susan Keller."[86]

Elizabeth and Jacob filed the inventory with the Commissary General on September 3, 1766, and it was sworn before T. Bowles, Deputy Commissary. As indicated, nearly four years elapsed until the filing of the final account.

This inventory and estate account raise some interesting questions. Assuming that the "Jacob Keller, deceased" was actually Jacob Koller, the father of Jacob The Elder, and that all these Kellers were actually Kollers, can they be fitted into a pattern?

Remember that Jacob The Elder bought 102 acres

---

[85] Frederick County Administrative Account B2-118.
[86] Frederick County Inventories, B2-195/196.

of RAMSHORN in 1750 and apparently owned no other land until he bought 100 acres of DEN OF WOLVES in 1754. It would seem rather obvious that he lived on RAMSHORN for at least four years, and since he was known in all his land transactions as a "farmer," he must certainly have had a house and some farm buildings — which may have been on the land when he bought it from Rhodes.

Remember also that he had RAMSHORN resurveyed in February 1765, but it was not patented to him until September 1765. It would scarcely seem likely that he would have built on any unowned part of RAMSHORN before he received his patent thereto. One of the items in the 1765 inventory is "grain in the field and in the barn, £13/16/9." The barn referred to seems most certainly to have been built before late in 1765.

Was the Jacob Keller who died in 1765 living on the 102-acre original purchase? And, when Jacob The Elder deeded 100 acres to Elizabeth in 1768, was he giving her title to the home in which she may have lived for some years? If so, it would most certainly indicate a father-son relationship between the two Jacob. But, unfortunately, a platting of the two tracts — Rhodes to Keller and Jacob to Elizabeth — produces very dissimilar tracts of land.

On the other hand, I think there is little doubt that the Jacob Keller who died in 1765 lived at least in the immediate vicinity of RAMSHORN. One evidence of this is Henry Fister's connection with the inventory and final account. He was one of the appraisers of the estate, and the administrators paid him £3/5/0, which I strongly suspect was for making a coffin — for he was a carpenter. The only other disbursement — except for court costs — was £7 to Mary Burge, purpose unstated.

There was a Henry Fister, carpenter, who on July 26, 1765 sold 30 acres of ALMOST NIGHT, which lay "at the head of the long meadow, a draft of Kitocton Creek."[87] The same Henry Fister, carpenter,

112

on April 12, 1770 bought 17 acres "on the north side of a draught of Mill Creek descending from Kitoctin Mountain."[88] Mill Creek was another name for Little Catoctin Creek. Both these Feaster properties were apparently very close to RAMSHORN.

While thus far there is only a strong circumstantial probability that "Jacob Keller, deceased 1765" is actually Jacob Koller, father of Jacob The Elder, that probability is strengthened by the fact that there is no evidence now available indicating the presence of any Kellers in the locality of RAMSHORN at that time. They all seem to have arrived later than 1765.

One more bit of evidence is even more intriguingly circumstantial. The total gross estate amounted to £164/13/0 — later reduced through disbursements to £125/2/9 — to one third of which, under her right of dower, Elizabeth would be entitled. One-third of the gross estate would amount to £54/17/8. Reference to Jacob's deed to Elizabeth on June 22, 1768 indicates the consideration for the 100 acres of RAMSHORN was £54. I had frequently speculated about that odd amount. Was it that Jacob said to her that for her share of his father's gross estate (the net was probably not known in 1768) he would deed her 100 acres of land? Actually it wasn't such a bad deal after all, for five years later Elizabeth Keller Smith sold the land to Jacob's son John for £260.

Jacob's half[?]-brother Andrew would also be entitled to a third of the estate, unless Susan, who witnessed the inventory and whom I can't yet identify, was a sister. But Jacob was much more generous to Andrew than to his step[?]-mother. He deeded Andrew 100 acres for only "love and affection."

Does all this find for the Cullers an ancestor one generation older than anyone has heretofore suspected? I strongly believe that it does!

---

[87] Frederick County Land Records, J-1257.
[88] Ibid., N-64.

RAMSHORN
RESURVEY ON RAMSHORN

Acquisitions

RAMSHORN was situated about one mile south of present-day Myersville. Dr. Grace L. Tracey in her manuscript, "Notes from the Records of Old Monocacy," states that RAMSHORN was surveyed March 10, 1739 for Daniel Dulany for 494 acres. This acreage is confirmed by two deeds: 102 acres by Henry Rod (Rhodes) and wife Catherine to Jacob Keller (so indexed) for a consideration of £125, recorded in Land Records B-341 under date of March 18, 1750; and 392 acres by John George Arnold to Daniel Arnold, recorded in Land Records E-61 under date of January 15, 1753. Rod is called Rhodes in this latter deed, which excepts "that part of it [RAMSHORN] that should run into a tract called THE HOGYARD conveyed to Samuel Arnold" by deed of this same date.

Rod's deed to Jacob Keller (Koller) transfers "all that tract or parcel of land called ROD'S PURCHASE, being part of a tract of land called RAMSHORN." It further recites that the tract was "patented in the name of John George Arnold."

On February 26, 1765 Jacob Keller (Koller) had his part of RAMSHORN resurveyed, adding 710 acres of vacant contiguous land, giving him a total of 812 acres, which was patented to him September 2, 1765. The land is described in the Patent as "of our Manor of Conococheague." However, the total RAMSHORN acreage conveyed by the five deeds recorded in June 1768 was 660. A platting of these five parcels on the whole tract indicates that the original 102 acres and possibly certain parts of Catoctin Creek (which flows through the land) were not transferred.

Dispositions
(All Indexed as Jacob Keller)

Liber, folio	Date	Conveyed to	Acres	Consid.	Jacob's wife's name shown as
L-361	6/22/1768[1]	*Elizabeth Keller, widow (his mother?)	100	£54	Mary
L-362	6/22/1768[1] 5/28/1768[2]	*John Keller	150	£10	Mary
L-364	6/22/1768[1]	*Andrew Keller, "a brother of said Jacob Keller"	100	Note[3]	Mary
L-365	6/22/1768[1] 5/28/1768[2]	John Arnold	226	£145/16	Mary
L-372	6/24/1768[1] 5/31/1768[2]	Peter Bainbridge	84	£56/19/6	Not mentioned

(This conveyed "End of Strife" and "Part of Resurvey on Ramshorn" as "obtained by Jacob Keller.")

Totals: 660 £266+

[1] Date recorded.
[2] Date of deed.
[3] "Love and affection" and "for the better maintenance and livelihood of said Andrew Keller."
* These deeds and that to Michael Keller (Culler) for DEN OF WOLVES (see page 116) are marked as follows on the deed record in the Court House:

John Keller's deed - "delivered to his brother"
Andrew Keller's deed - "delivered to his mother"
Elizabeth Keller's deed - "delivered" (i.e., to herself)
Michael Keller's deed - "delivered" (i.e., to himself)

I interpret this to indicate that Elizabeth was Andrew's mother, that she took delivery of his deed along with her own and that Michael was John's brother and he took delivery of John's deed along with his own. (See text.)

114

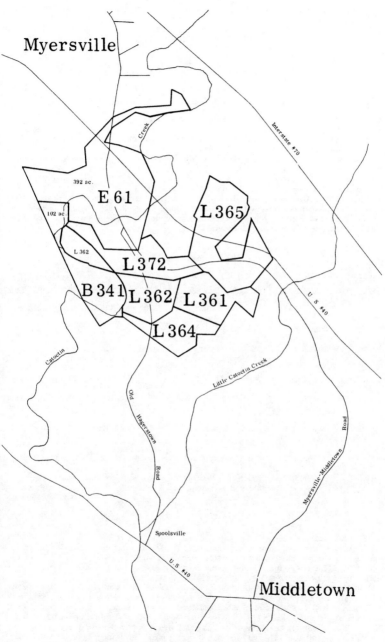

Myersville

392 ac.

E 61

L 365

102 ac.

L 362

L 372

B 341 L 362 L 361

L 364

Creek

Interstate #70

U S #40

Catoctin

Old Hagerstown Road

Little Catoctin Creek

Myersville-Middletown Road

Spoolsville

U S #40

Middletown

RESURVEY ON RAMSHORN

115

DEN OF WOLVES
RESURVEY ON DEN OF WOLVES

Acquisitions
(All Indexed as Jacob Keller)

Liber, folio	Date	Conveyed by	Acres	Consid.
E-421	4/25/1754	George Honey	100	£65

DEN OF WOLVES was surveyed for George Honey for 100 acres on March 3, 1742 and was patented to him on April 24, 1754.

On November 10, 1761 DEN OF WOLVES was resurveyed for Jacob Keller (Koller) for 777 acres and was patented to him on September 29, 1762. I do not have the Maryland Land Office reference for this resurvey, but it is referred to in Liber RP-177, Frederick County Land Records, under date of August 18, 1777.

RESURVEY ON DEN OF WOLVES extended approximately from the present town of Lewistown northeastward to the vicinity of Hunting Creek, and parts of present-day Angleberger and Bottomley Roads were included within it. Honey's original 100 acres was the northeasternmost part of the Resurvey.

Dispositions
(All Indexed as Jacob Keller)

Liber, folio	Date	Conveyed to	Acres	Consid.	Jacob's wife's name shown as
K-1357	6/22/1767	Nicholas Knezer (Knezell, Kenezott)	200	£100	Mary (Collier)
	(Signed by mark: Jacob Collier)				
L-360	6/22/1768	Michael Keller (Culler)	100	£ 20	Mary
L-361	6/22/1768	John Smith	100	£ 50	Mary
U-415	12/17/1773 (Jacob Collier)	Christian Shryoch	2+	£ 3	Not mentioned
V-516	5/26/1774 (Jacob Collar)	Robert Wood	17	£ 43/6	Magdalin
RP-176	8/18/1777	Christopher Gough	35¾	£ 62	Mary Magdaline
§RP-177	8/18/1777	Frederick William Shriver of York Co., Pennsylvania	200	£925	Space in deed for wife's name not filled in.
		Totals:	654¾	£1203/6	

§ - Recites that the parties agree (without survey) that part of RESURVEY ON DEN OF WOLVES "does not clear of elder surveys" and states that they estimate "all residue and undisposed parts" to contain 200 acres. (Therefore, if the original Resurvey contained 777 acres, since the foregoing conveyances total 654¾+ acres, it was foul of elder surveys by approximately 122 acres.)

Recites further that "John Keller, son of....Jacob Keller, now resident on the premises" shall "quietly....enjoy and possess the house wherein he now lives, together with half the garden, two acres of meadow and three acres of upland, clear of rent....until the first day of April next [1778]." Also, that John Smith, "at this time tenant of Jacob Keller," shall remain on the land for two years from September 30, 1777, paying rent to Shriver as follows: £18 (current money) per year, plus 10 pounds of hackled flax."

Plat of RESURVEY ON DEN OF WOLVES

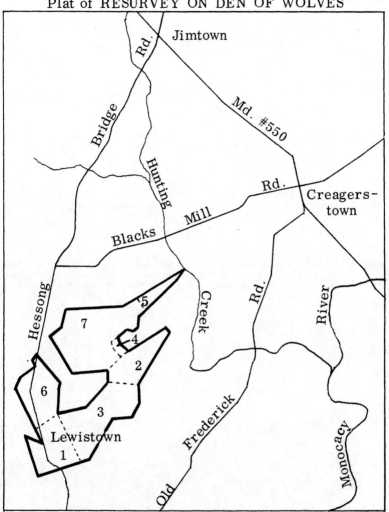

Numbers show location of the several tracts sold:
1 Michael Keller [Culler]   L-360
2 John Smith   L-361
3 Nicholas Knezer   K-1357
4 Christian Shryoch   U-415
5 Robert Wood   V-516
6 Christopher Gough   RP-176
7 Frederick William Shriver   RP-177

Real Estate Transactions of Jacob Koller (Coller) "The Elder" - Cont'd.

OTHER TRANSACTIONS

Acquisitions

Liber, folio	Date	
RP-146	7/20/1777	To Jacob Goller from Philip Grantler half of Lot No. 136 in Frederick City. Consideration £40. Lot size, 30 x 393 feet. Subject to Ground Rent of £1 yearly, payable to Daniel Dulany.
RP-354	4/21/1778	To Jacob Goller from Jacob Bentz Lot No. 13 in "the addition Frederick Town formerly laid out by a certain Caspar Myers, late deceased, ...being part of.... Long Acre....being part of ....Tasker's Chance." Consideration £70.

Dispositions

WR 2-624	6/25/1780	Jacob Coller, "farmer of Frederick County, to George Jacob Baltzell, tailor," half of Lot No. 136 in Frederick City. Consideration £2000. Jacob's wife shown as Magdalena. Jacob is called Goller in body of deed and at signature by mark.
WR 7-123	1/25/1787	Jacob Culler (so indexed and so spelled in deed) to John Culler, his son, both of Shenandoah County, Virginia, Lot No. 13, above. Consideration £15 (note reduction). Jacob's wife's name not shown. Jacob appointed "my trusty friend, Lawrence Delauter, of Shenandoah County, Virginia" to go to Frederick County, Maryland and vouch for Jacob's signature to the deed.

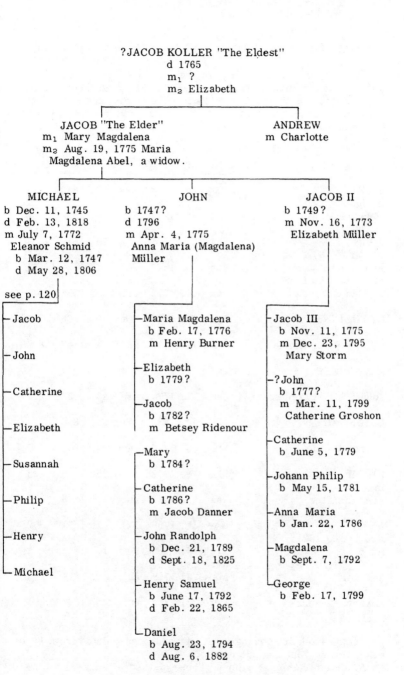

?JACOB KOLLER "The Eldest"
d 1765
m₁ ?
m₂ Elizabeth

JACOB "The Elder"
m₁ Mary Magdalena
m₂ Aug. 19, 1775 Maria
Magdalena Abel, a widow.

ANDREW
m Charlotte

MICHAEL
b Dec. 11, 1745
d Feb. 13, 1818
m July 7, 1772
Eleanor Schmid
b Mar. 12, 1747
d May 28, 1806

see p. 120

– Jacob

– John

– Catherine

– Elizabeth

– Susannah

– Philip

– Henry

– Michael

JOHN
b 1747?
d 1796
m Apr. 4, 1775
Anna Maria (Magdalena)
Müller

–Maria Magdalena
b Feb. 17, 1776
m Henry Burner

–Elizabeth
b 1779?

–Jacob
b 1782?
m Betsey Ridenour

–Mary
b 1784?

– Catherine
b 1786?
m Jacob Danner

– John Randolph
b Dec. 21, 1789
d Sept. 18, 1825

– Henry Samuel
b June 17, 1792
d Feb. 22, 1865

–Daniel
b Aug. 23, 1794
d Aug. 6, 1882

JACOB II
b 1749?
m Nov. 16, 1773
Elizabeth Müller

– Jacob III
b Nov. 11, 1775
m Dec. 23, 1795
Mary Storm

–?John
b 1777?
m Mar. 11, 1799
Catherine Groshon

–Catherine
b June 5, 1779

–Johann Philip
b May 15, 1781

–Anna Maria
b Jan. 22, 1786

–Magdalena
b Sept. 7, 1792

–George
b Feb. 17, 1799

119

CHILDREN OF MICHAEL AND ELEANOR (SMITH) CULLER

Michael, born Dec. 11, 1745, died Feb. 13, 1818, married July 7, 1772[1] Eleanor Smith, born Mar. 12, 1747, died May 28, 1806. Both are buried in the Culler Family Cemetery on the old Culler farm near Jefferson on the east side of Holter Road, three-fourths of a mile north of its intersection with Maryland Route #180.

	Born[2]	Died[2]	Where Buried[3]
JACOB	May 25, 1773[4]	Aug. 2, 1843[4]	3
m June 2, 1802			
Barbara Long	Apr. 25, 1777	Sept. 9, 1856	3
JOHN	*Oct. 11, 1774	Mar. 19, 1847	1
m[1] Aug. 16, 1804			
Mary Ann Coblentz	Jan. 5, 1778	Sept. 14, 1824	1
m[2] Sept. 12, 1827			
Juliann Coblentz	Jan. 14, 1772	July 25, 1854	2
CATHERINE	*Dec. 20, 1776	Mar. 30, 1866	5
m Nov. 24, 1797			
George Peter Ramsburg	Mar. 16, 1770	July 4, 1847	5
ELIZABETH	*Oct. 17, 1778	Feb. 7, 1857	4
m May 19, 1802			
John P[hilip] Coblentz	Jan. 1, 1776	Jan. 28, 1853	4
SUSANNAH	Mar. 14, 1781	May 24, 1864	2
m June 8, 1805			
George Willard	May 13, 1770	Dec. 24, 1849	2
PHILIP	*May 8, 1783	Feb. 25, 1855	3
m			
Mary Feaster	Jan. 5, 1787	July 8, 1845	3
HENRY	*Nov. 10, 1786	Feb. 1, 1861	2
m Apr. 6, 1809[1]			
Anna Feaster	Aug. 17, 1789	Dec. 16, 1856	2
MICHAEL	*Mar. 25, 1789	July 28, 1874	3
m Sept. 27, 1819			
Barbara Thomas	Feb. 22, 1795	July 23, 1873	3

[1] Actual dates of marriage. Others are license dates from Frederick County Marriage Records.

[2] All dates from gravestones. Those marked with asterisk (*) are corroborated by early Lutheran Church Records.

³ Key to burial locales:
1 Culler Family Cemetery, near Jefferson, Maryland.
2 Lutheran Cemetery, Jefferson, Maryland.
3 Mt. Zion Cemetery, near Lucas, Ohio.
4 Reformed Church Cemetery, Middletown, Maryland.
5 Cemetery on old Thomas farm, near Adamstown, Maryland.
⁴ I have listed Jacob first above because, along with some other members of the family, I think he was Michael's oldest child. Since both of Jacob's grandfathers were named Jacob (Jacob Culler and Jacob Smith), it was most natural for Michael and Eleanor to name their first-born Jacob. How better could they please both?

Moreover, in his will Michael mentions all his children in the order of their birth, grouping sons first and then the daughters. Jacob is named first in the list of sons.

But when I attempt to determine the date of Jacob's birth, I encounter difficulties. Mr. John P. Dern, who searched the original Frederick Lutheran records for me, cannot find Jacob's birth. His gravestone records his death as August 2, 1845 and states he was aged 70 years, 2 months and 8 days. Simple subtraction, therefore indicates his birth date as May 24, 1775. But John, whose birth date is corroborated by the church records, was born October 11, 1774, making the interval between them an implausible seven months.

Mr. Fred H. Crone (now deceased) of Santa Paula, California a great-grandson of Jacob, gave his birth date as February 8, 1775, providing an impossible interval.

However, from an equity case dated December 25, 1843, involving the estate of Jacob's father-in-law John Long, we learn that the latter's daughter Barbara was by then already a widow. (Frederick County Equity Record WBT 2-409, Case #1919.) Hence the stonecutter must have erred in cutting a death date for Jacob of 1845 instead of 1843. It is my conclusion, therefore, that Jacob died Aug. 2, 184<u>3</u> and so was born May 25, 177<u>3</u>. This would be quite logical in view of his parents' marriage in July 1772 and the expected interval until John's birth in October 1774.

John Long's wife, Margaret Flook, is buried in the Flook Cemetery near Middletown. John is buried in the Middletown Lutheran Cemetery. Their house on LONG'S LAST CHANCE, midway between Jefferson and Burkittsville, still stands. The names of Long's children are listed in the Equity Record cited above.

CHILDREN OF CAPT. HENRY AND ANNA (FEASTER) CULLER

All marriage dates are date of license from the Frederick County Marriage Records, except for Daniel, whose date is date of ceremony.

	Born	Died	Where Buried[1]
DANIEL	Mar. 9, 1810	Mar. 4, 1894	2
m Apr. 13, 1836			
Ann Maria Hargett	Aug. 19, 1815	Jan. 2, 1891	2
PHILIP	Nov. 2, 1811	May 20, 1884	2
m Sept. 23, 1844			
Ann R. Dixon	Oct. 10, 1825	July 19, 1908	2
DAVID	Jan. 2, 1814	Jan. 20, 1881	2
m June 9, 1858			
Margaret Ann Slifer	July 31, 1833	May 28, 1903	2
AN INFANT CHILD	Nov. 9, 1815	Nov. 23, 1815	1
Col. HENRY	May 29, 1817	Mar. 7, 1902	2
m₁ Feb. 4, 1845			
Eliza A. Warfield	Mar. 16, 1817	Jan. 22, 1873	2
m₂			
Mrs. Harriett L. Sowers	June 26, 1833	July 6, 1911	2
MICHAEL	Apr. 7, 1820	1898	2
m Apr. 20, 1846			
Elizabeth Toms	1826	1897	2
Dr. JOHN JACOB	Nov. 28, 1822	Mar. 13, 1900	2
m Sept. 22, 1852			
Sarah Ann Routzahn	Dec. 1, 1829	June 30, 1902	2
GEORGE W.	May 8, 1825	July 11, 1826	1
SAMUEL CLAY	June 30, 1827	Aug. 4, 1832	1
WILLIAM LUTHER	Apr. 12, 1831	Feb. 2, 1917	2
m₁ May 18, 1855			
Mary Minerva Hawker	Jan. 24, 1838	Apr. 6, 1886	2
m₂			
Allie LeFay (of Missouri)			?

---

[1] Key to burial locales:
1 Culler Family Cemetery, near Jefferson, Maryland
2 Lutheran Cemetery, Jefferson, Maryland

CHILDREN OF DANIEL AND ANN MARIA (HARGETT) CULLER

Marriage dates are taken from my Mother's Family Bible.

	Born	Died	Where Buried[1]
JOHN HENRY	Jan. 30, 1838	Sept. 26, 1911	6
m Mar. 20, 1866			
Amanda A. Derr	Apr. 12, 1839	Aug. 20, 1914	6
Rev. MARTIN LUTHER	Oct. 13, 1839	Aug. 10, 1925	7
m Oct. 26, 1865			
Mary Jane Floyd		Jan. 3, 1913	7
MARY ANN CATHERINE	July 7, 1841	Aug. 11, 1882	6
m Dec. 12, 1860			
George W. Slagle	Sept. 23, 1833	May 20, 1893	6
ELLEN REBECCA	Aug. 21, 1843	Dec. 15, 1891	8
m May 15, 1866			
William H. Howard	July 13, 1836	May 30, 1855	8
ANN VIRGINIA	Jan. 19, 1846	Oct. 13, 1871	4
m Feb. 19, 1867			
D. Edward Kefauver	Sept. 13, 1841	Dec. 11, 1922	4
AMERICA ELIZA	Jan. 25, 1848	May 2, 1919	6
m Mar. 24, 1874			
Carlton R. Horine	May 30, 1848	Feb. 2, 1930	6
DANIEL MILTON	May 11, 1850	Dec. 28, 1896	9
m Feb. 17, 1876			
Catherine R. Horine	Jan. 25, 1855	Apr. 10, 1928	9
MARIA ELIZABETH	Jan. 15, 1853	Apr. 9, 1914	6
m Sept. 12, 1893			
Milton Grove Rice	Nov. 11, 1844	Mar. 23, 1926	6
MILLARD FILLMORE	Dec. 27, 1855	Mar. 12, 1928	6
m Mar. 1, 1881			
Annie C. Remsburg	1855	Apr. 24, 1912	6

[1] Key to burial locales:
4 Reformed Church Cemetery, Middletown, Maryland
6 Union Cemetery, Jefferson, Maryland
7 Mercersburg, Pennsylvania
8 Mt. Olivet Cemetery, Frederick, Maryland
9 St. Luke Lutheran Cemetery, Feagaville, Maryland

CULLER FAMILY GRAVEYARD

Located on the old Culler farm near Jefferson, Maryland, on the east side of Holter Road, about three-fourths of a mile north of State Route #180. Epitaphs are keyed to the numbers shown on the following plat, which is not drawn to scale.

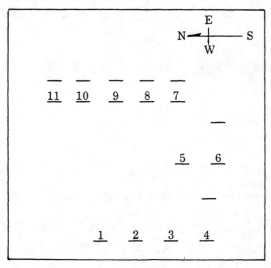

Holter Road, Jefferson to Middletown

1

HIER RUHET
LINORA COLLER[n]
GEBOR[n] 12 MERZ 1747
GEST[n] 28 May 1806

2

HIER
RUHED LENORA COLLER[n]
Gebohren Den 12th Merz 1747
Gestorben Dec 28th May 1806 Ist ALd
Worden 59 Iahr & 2 Monden & 16 Dag.

3

HIER
RUHET MICHAE[l]
KOLLER
Ist gebohrenden
11th Decembr 1745
gestorben den 13th
Februari 1818 ist
alt worten 72 Iah[r]
2 Mondt und 2 dags

4

In Memory of
ELEANOR CULLER
who was born Jan[y] 15th 1807
and died Sept[r] 2[d] 1823
Aged 16 years 7 months
and 17 days

5

HIER
Ruhet E Lisabeth CoLLe
rin Gebohren Den 8th Sep
Tember 1811 Gestorben Den
24 August 1815 Ist ALT
Worten 3 Iahr 11 Monad
Und 15 dags

6

In
Memory of
MARY ANN CULLER
Who was Born January 5th
1778 And Departed this
life September 14th 1824
Aged 46 Years 8 Months
and 9 Days

7

In Memory Of
JOHN CULLER
born Oct. 11, 1774
& died March 19, 1847
Aged 72 Years
5 months & 8 days

8

IN
Memory Of
GEORGE W.
son of Henry and
Anna Culler born
8th May 1825
& died 11th July 1826

9

IN
Memory of
JOSEPH CULLER
who was Born
June 7th 1823 and
Departed this life
September 18th
1824. Aged 1 Year
3 months and
11 days

10

IN
MEMORY Of
An infant child of
HENRY and ANNA
CULLER born 9th
Nov. 1815. Aged
14 days

11

SAMUEL CLAY
son of
HENRY & Anna
CULLER
Born June 30, 1827
Died Aug. 4, 1832
Aged 5 years 1 mo
& 4 days

This Indenture made the Twenty Second Day of August One Thousand Seven Hundred and Seventy Seven Between John Conrad Teboe of Dunmore County and Colony of Virginia of the one part and John Hoeller Late of Frederick County in the Colony of Maryland of the other part, Witness that the said John Conrad Teboe for and in consideration of the sum of five Shillings Current Money to him in hand paid by the said John Hoeller at or before the Sealing and Delivery of these presents, Doth grant bargain and sell to the said John Hoeller a Certain Tract or Parcell of Land situate lying & Being in Dunmore County on Passage Creek in Powell's fort and bounded as by a Survey Thereof made by Robert Rutherford, Beginning on the East side of said Creek at two Hicorys and two white oak saplins near the end of a small point between two Drains and Extending No. 2.5 W. fifty Two poles to Edmund Baisies Corner a white Oak, black oak and wild cherry Trees, thence with this Line the Course Continued One Hundred and Eighty Eight poles crossing the said Creek to three white Oak saplins on the foot of a hill near a branch then Leaving Baisies's Line and Extending No. 2.4 E Two hundred and forty Poles to a pine on a hill Thence So. 2.5 E Two hundred and forty Poles crossing the said Creek to a stake near three white Oaks, Marked Corners on the brow of a small hill near a Drain and then So. 2.5 West Two hundred and forty Poles to the Beginning Containing Three hundred and Sixty Acres in this bounds, but the said John Conrad Teboe only sales grants and bargains Only Two hundred and fifty One Acres out of the three hundred & Sixty Acres, and all houses, buildings, Orchard ways, waters, Water Courses, Profits, Comodities Hereditaments and Appurtenances Whatsoever to the said Premises hereby granted or any portion thereof belonging to in any wise appertaining and the reversion & Reversions Remainder & Remainders Rents Issues, and profits thereof To have and To hold the Lands hereby conveyed and all and singular other the premises hereby Granted with the Appurtenances unto the said John Hoeller his Executors Administrators and Assigns from the Day before the Date hereof for and During the full Term and Time of our whole Year from thence next Ensuing fully to be Compleat and Ended Yielding and paying therefore the rent of one pepper Corn on Lady Day next: the same shall be Lawfully Demanded to the Intent and purpose that by Virtue of the presents and the Statute for Transferring uses into Possession the said John Hoeller may be in actual Possession of the Premises and be thereby Enabled to accept and Take a grant and Release of the Reversion and Inheritance thereof To him and his heirs. In Witness whereof the said John Conrad Teboe hath hereunto set his hand and seal the Day and Year first above Written.

Sealed and Delivered   John Conrad Teboe
in the Presence of   (Scroll for seal)
[omitted]

At a court held for Dunmore County the 26th day of August 1777. This Indenture was Acknowledged by Conrad Teboe Party thereto and Ordered to be Recorded.

Teste

Thomas Marshall C. D. C.

---

[1] This transcript by courtesy of Mr. W. E. Boyer, Cashier, The National Bank of Woodstock, Woodstock, Virginia.

GEORGE BALTUS DUTROW AND HIS FAMILY

Shortly after completing the preceding Culler
Family material in 1969, I made an intriguing discovery. I found that while a great-great-grandfather
on one side of my family, Michael Culler, had bought
approximately half of MATTHEWS GOOD WILL in
1776, a great-great-grandfather on the other side,
George Baltus Dutrow, had acquired the remainder
twenty-one years earlier and in 1798 had sold his part
to Michael Culler.

This whetted my interest in MATTHEWS GOOD
WILL and its division between my two ancestors. And
since apparently no one had recorded anything about
George Baltus Dutrow and his family, I undertook also
to learn something about that.

The result was the following brief sketch. In preparing it I constructed the accompanying plat (see page
134), part of which, with its notes, is also a supple-
ment to the Culler Family material.

* * *

The spelling of Dutrow has myriad variations in
the Land and Will records of Frederick County, Maryland. Some of them are: Dodrow, Dotroe, Duddero,
Duderoe, Dudrow, Dutteraer, Dutterer, Duttero,
Tutterah, Tuttero and Tutterow.

The earliest Dutrow I can now definitely connect
with Martha Dutrow Rice, my great-grandmother, is
George Baltus (Baldes, Baltice, etc.) Dutrow, her
father. Baltus and its variations are a corruption of
Balthasar, and I assume that his ancestry was Ger-

man. His first wife, whose given name was shown in 1769 as Dorcas,[1] was probably of English descent.

There is one other Dutrow who appears earlier in the Frederick County Land Records than does George Baltus. This is John Dutrow, whose name is spelled Dutteraer in the Land Office survey records and Dutterer in the earliest Frederick County Land record. On January 26, 1753 MATTHEWS GOOD WILL, consisting of 200 acres, was surveyed for John Dutteraer.[2] Two years later, on February 5, 1755, John sold for a consideration of £16 half of MATTHEWS GOOD WILL to Baltice Duttero — whom we know as George Baltus Dutrow.[3] I cannot now establish a relationship between John and Baltus, although I feel certain there was such, either fraternal or as father and son.

On March 26, 1771 John Dutrow sold the remaining 100 acres of MATTHEWS GOOD WILL to Conrad RAGHER for £130.[4] Thereafter John disappears from Frederick County records, and I know nothing further about him. In the 1771 deed John's wife is shown as Rosannah, a name much used in England. The marked difference in selling price for these two 100-acre tracts may indicate a price concession by John to a relative, although the tract sold to Ragher quite probably was much better improved than that sold to George Batlus.

In August 1776 Ragher sold his 100 acres to Michael Culler for £250. This tract is the original part of Culler's holdings in Middletown Valley and became what for more than a century was known as the "Old Culler Farm" on which is located the Culler Family Cemetery.[5]

---

[1] Frederick County Land Records, M-134.
[2] Maryland Land Office Patent Records, GS1-83.
[3] Frederick County Land Records, E-653.
[4] Ibid., O-109.
[5] For a description of the Dutrow and Culler lands, see accompanying Plat and Notes below, pp. 134-136.

Since George Baltus owned no other improved land, it seems rather obvious that he lived on his MATTHEWS GOOD WILL acreage from the time he bought it in 1755 until 1798 when he sold it to Michael Culler for £500.[6]

I am reasonably certain that the present (1975) Roy Remsburg Road was the approximate northern boundary of MATTHEWS GOOD WILL. Since Baltus Dutrow's land adjoined John Dutrow's on the west, I think George Baltus must have lived on the south side of that road somewhere between the "Old Culler Farm" and the present Roy Remsburg farm dwelling. If this assumption is correct, his dwelling and other buildings have long ago been razed and there is no present evidence where they were located.

Incidentally, the Roy Remsburg Road was a part of the first road from the mouth of the Monocacy to the Conococheague (Williamsport) area by way of Crampton's Gap (Gapland). The road was then known as "the Road to Israel Friend's Mill," and the present Teen Barnes Road led it westward over Catoctin Mountain. The road continued westward, probably along the small stream which borders it, to what is now known as Lewis' Mill — then known as Richard Touchstone's place — and westward from there. It later became known as "the Road by way of Richard Touchstone's."[7]

In 1758 George Baltus, for £30, bought 56 acres of GRAVELLY SPRING from William Keesey (Keeser).[8] He sold this same acreage for £30 to Thomas Taylor in March of 1769.[9] Taylor owned PILE HALL, whose 366 acres had a common beginning with MATTHEWS GOOD WILL and adjoined it on the north. Taylor was an English land speculator who bought and sold numerous tracts in Frederick County and in Loudoun County,

---

[6] Frederick County Land Records, WR 16-392.
[7] See above, pp. 55-59.
[8] Frederick County Land Records, F-284.
[9] Ibid., M-134.

Virginia.   He died in the late 1790s in Virginia.

The deed to Taylor shows Baltus' wife's name as Dorcas.   The identical purchase and sale prices indicate little or no improvements on the land, and I suspect it may have been mountain land which lay on the east side of Catoctin Mountain, for its beginning point is described as "near the head of a spring that runs into the south branch of Ballenger's Creek."   This spring is probably that designated as Keesey's Spring in a 1748 deed from Matthews to Davis.[10]

I do not know when Dorcas Dutrow died, but by a license dated October 29, 1784 Baltus married Elizabeth Slagle, a widow with seven children, who was undoubtedly considerably his junior.   Since George Baltus was at that time at least 50 years old, the addition of seven minor children to his family was something of an undertaking.

Elizabeth Slagle was probably the widow of one Henry Slagle who died intestate some time between 1780 and 1784 and whose modest estate was administered by an Elizabeth Slagle in 1784.

I cannot further identify this Henry Slagle. However, so far as I can find in the records, he never owned land in Frederick County.   The Slagles apparently came into Maryland from Pennsylvania, and Elizabeth and Henry may have been among such early arrivals.   At least two Slagles, Christopher and Daniel, are found in early Frederick County land records, selling land which they apparently acquired before the formation of Frederick County.   Christopher is described as "of the Province of Pensylvany," and Daniel as "of York County, Pennsylvania."

In 1802 George Baltus bought approximately 232 acres, consisting of four or more tracts, from Levy and John Hughes for a price in excess of £1,200.[11] Possibly he rented this land during the interval from

---

[10]   Ibid., B-2.
[11]   Ibid., WR 23-302, 331.

1798 to 1802. Since there is no other obvious reason for this purchase of larger acreage, it was probable that he found the 89 acres[12] of MATTHEWS GOOD WILL (he had sold one acre to Jacob Feaster in 1796) too small to support his large family. Moreover, with his step-children reaching maturity, there was greater opportunity to use their labor productively. Shortly after his purchase he sold 50 acres to Benjamin Rice and in 1806 had the remaining acreage resurveyed into one tract called CATOCTIN RIDGE.[13]

CATOCTIN RIDGE lay on the high east bank of Catoctin Creek, about a mile south of present US #340. The only part of it of which I know present (1975) ownership is an indefinite acreage owned by Lane Skinner.[14]

I do not know when George Baltus Dutrow was born, but assuming that as a minor he could not have held title to the land he bought from John in 1755, he could not have been born later than 1734. I do know, however, that he died on March 1, 1808. This I learn from an Equity proceeding begun in August 1826.[15]

His will was dated August 3, 1803 and was probated March 9, 1808.[16] In it he left all his property to his second wife, Elizabeth Slagle Dutrow, for her lifetime or until her remarriage. He provided at Elizabeth's death his remaining estate should be distributed as shown below. He named Elizabeth and Benjamin Rice as executors.[17]

---

[12] A 1763 resurvey had reduced the original 100 acres to 90, out of which one acre was sold to Jacob Feaster in 1796. See below, pp. 134-136.
[13] Frederick County Survey Records, THO 1-355.
[14] Frederick County Land Records, 701-300.
[15] Frederick County Equity Records, JS 5-615 et seq.
[16] Frederick County Will Records, GMRB 1-365.
[17] About 1792 Benjamin Rice built what is now known as Bell's Mill, situated near where Maryland State Route #464 crosses Catoctin Creek.

George Baltus Dutrow devised his estate thus:

£10 to his daughter Elizabeth, wife of John Thrasher, whom she had married by a license dated September 29, 1783. Elizabeth died before 1826, at which time Thrasher was living in Kentucky.

£25 to his daughter "Darkey," quite obviously Dorcas, named for her mother. She never married and was dead before 1826.

£30/10 sh. to his daughter Catherine, wife of George Renn.

£37/10 sh. to his daughter "Pady," a pet name for Martha, the wife of Perry G. Rice, Sr., whom she had married in 1794.

£15 to Sally (Sarah) Willing, whom he doesn't call "daughter" in his will. She married Jacob Rhodes.

£10 to Thomas Winfield, who is not called a "son."

All his real estate to his sons George Baltus, Jr., and Isaac, with right of survivorship. Isaac died January 1, 1816 without issue, so that all the real estate devolved to George Baltus, Jr., at the death of Elizabeth Slagle Dutrow.

Elizabeth Slagle Dutrow died in October of 1823.[18] Her will was dated February 26, 1822 and was probated October 7, 1823.[19] In it she undertook to distribute the personal property of the estate, which was rather substantial, to the seven children she had by her first husband. Her argument was that, since George Baltus Dutrow's death she had paid so many of his debts, all his personal property now belonged to her absolutely to do with as she pleased. I am skeptical of this argument, since I find nothing in the records to indicate that George Baltus was other than fully solvent at his death.

The Slagle children mentioned in Elizabeth's will were John, Mary McClary, Frederick, Elizabeth Kel-

---

[18] Frederick County Equity Records, JS5-615.
[19] Frederick County Will Records, HS3-209.

ler, Charles, Henry and Jacob. She appointed "my two sons, George Baltes Duderoe and Henry Slagle" as her executors. And as directed by her husband's will, she devised the real estate to George B. Dutrow, Jr., and Isaac Dutrow, even though Isaac had died in 1816.

The mentioning of "my two sons" raises the interesting question whether Isaac was a son of Dorcas while George, Jr., was actually Elizabeth's son. George, Jr., married Ruth Rice (daughter of Benjamin) in 1812, and if he was Elizabeth's son, he would have been about 27 years old — a normal marriageable age. If he was Dorcas' son, he would have been marrying rather late in life.[20]

George B. Dutrow, Jr., died intestate in 1826. His affairs were evidently much involved, for in January of 1825 he made an assignment to Henry and Frederick Slagle for the benefit of his creditors. As a result of the Equity proceeding mentioned above, the whole of CATOCTIN RIDGE was sold by John Nelson, Trustee, to John H. and Cornelia Hilleary,[21] who in 1829 sold $31\frac{1}{4}$ acres to James Torrence[22] and in 1832 sold $10\frac{1}{4}$ acres to Lloyd Gittings.[23]

Since George Baltus Dutrow, Sr., apparently had only two sons, Isaac and George B., Jr., and since Isaac died without issue, any male descendants of George, Sr., carrying forward his family name would be the sons of George, Jr. The latter's children were Reuben, Ruth, Elizabeth Hook, James, Jemimah, Rebeccah, John and George. I have searched at some

---

[20] Note that daughters Elizabeth and Martha married in 1783 and 1794, respectively.
[21] Frederick County Equity Records, JS5-639; Frederick County Land Records, JS32-12.
[22] Ibid., JS31-431.
[23] Ibid., JS 38-173. Anyone interested in tracing other parts of CATOCTIN RIDGE will find a starting point in Frederick County Land Records, WBT 1-149.

length for a clue to the fate of the sons of George, Jr., but thus far in vain. Remembering that his wife was Benjamin Rice's daughter and that after Benjamin's death in 1820 his two sons, John Clifford and James, migrated to Ohio, I feel it is quite probable that after the death of her husband, Ruth also went to Ohio with her children.

DUTROW-CULLER PLAT

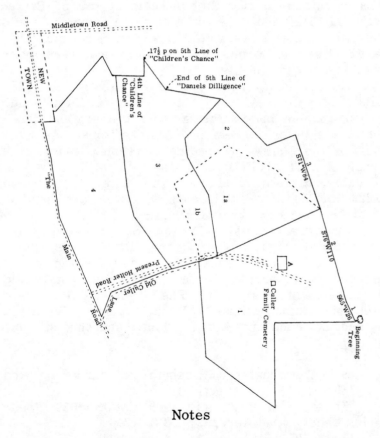

Notes

<u>1</u>, <u>1a</u> & <u>1b</u>: These three tracts comprise the original MATTHEWS GOOD WILL as surveyed and granted to John Dutteraer in 1753 for 200 acres. They probably

did not contain a full 200 acres as surveyed, for in 1763 part <u>1b</u>, 20 acres, was found to be foul of an older survey. The original survey states that the beginning tree is also the beginning tree of PILE HALL.

<u>1a</u> & <u>1b</u> were sold by John Dutteraer as 100 acres to Baltice Duttero in 1755 (E-653). Baltice (George Baltus) Dutrow had a resurvey made in 1763, which added <u>2</u>, 36 acres of vacant land. <u>1a</u> at that time was shown as containing only 54 acres. After the resurvey George B. Dutrow owned <u>1a</u> & <u>2</u>, said by the surveyor to contain 90 acres.

<u>1</u>: John Dutteraer sold this to Conrad Ragher in 1771 as 100 acres (O-109). In 1776 Ragher sold this to Michael Culler (BD2-338).

<u>1b</u> & <u>3</u>: Meanwhile, Michael Culler had acquired these two tracts containing $105\frac{1}{4}$ acres. In 1791 Culler and Francis Hoffman (owner of <u>4</u>) recorded a boundary agreement (WR9-675) in which owners of contiguous properties also joined. The outlines of the Culler and Hoffman properties are here platted from the courses and distances in that agreement.

<u>1a</u> & <u>2</u>: In 1798 George B. Dutrow sold this land to Michael Culler. As noted in the text, this was a sale by a great-great-grandfather on my father's side to a great-great-grandfather on my mother's side. After 1798 Michael Culler owned all tracts shown, except <u>4</u>. In 1810 he had a resurvey (THO1-296) incorporating most or all of these lands, plus some others, which totaled 269 acres and which he then called FAIR DAY. Michael's son Henry acquired <u>4</u> after Michael's death.

<u>A</u>: This is the approximate location of the house and buildings of the Ragher-Culler part of MATTHEWS GOOD WILL and their present location as well.

<u>Holter Road</u>: This road is modern and is drawn in merely as a land-mark.

<u>The Main Road</u>: This is the title given in the 1791 Hoffman-Culler Agreement, and it is platted on the courses and distances given therein.

<u>Old Culler Lane</u>: This is my arbitrary name for this very old road which was closed when Holter Road was

built. I consider the Lane something of a mystery. It is deeply worn, indicating both age and considerable use. Yet it doesn't appear on any map, either Varle's 1808 map or the 1873 Atlas. A very old road, shown on old maps but now closed, leading around the mountain and joining others leading to the Mouth of the Monocacy River, comes out on the Frederick Road about a quarter of a mile east of Culler Lane. I have long speculated that these two roads may have led into Israel Friends-Roy Remsburg Road by a much easier route than the Teen Barnes Road.

THE EARLIEST YEARS OF MIDDLETOWN

In his History of Western Maryland, Scharf[1] states that Middletown was "laid out just after the close of the Revolution by Margaret Crone, who owned the land on which the town now stands." Williams and McKinsey, in their History of Frederick County,[2] repeat this almost verbatim and add some details.

They state that Middletown was laid out on a tract of land called SMITHFIELD, which derived its name from a gunsmith shop built on it in 1730 by one Frederick Lauber "near where the residence of Mr. Charles Butts....now [1910] stands."

Unfortunately for the reliability of the foregoing, Frederick County Court, Land and Will Records reveal an entirely different story.

On August 4, 1750 a Land Warrant for 100 acres was granted Notley Thomas, and on November 25, 1750 Thomas assigned 50 acres of this warrant to Richard Smith.

However, in anticipation of this assignment, 44 acres had been surveyed on October 10, 1750 for Smith by Isaac Brooke, Deputy Surveyor for Maryland, and was called, quite logically, SMITHFIELD. Smith's patent was effective from the date of the survey. Incidentally, there is nothing in the land records to in-

---

[1] J. Thomas Scharf, History of Western Maryland (Philadelphia, 1882), vol. 1, p. 574.
[2] T. J. C. Williams and Folger McKinsey, History of Frederick County, Maryland (Hagerstown, 1910), vol. 1, pp. 323, 499-500.

dicate that Frederick Lauber ever owned land in Frederick County.

SMITHFIELD was laid off in what might be termed a "hole" of vacant land surrounded by older surveys. On the south and west of SMITHFIELD lay WATSON'S WELFARE and on the east were CHEVY CHASE and TURKEY RANGE. Since 1750 there have been so many surveys and resurveys of tracts surrounding SMITHFIELD and so many claims and counterclaims based thereon, that it is impossible to determine the priority and validity of most of them. Apparently, however, only WATSON'S WELFARE affected the early boundaries of SMITHFIELD.

As early as 1742 Notley Thomas had a survey made north of present-day Point of Rocks. There is no indication of his relationship with Richard Smith, nor whether the assignment of the partial warrant of 50 acres was for a consideration or was a gift. It seems rather obvious, however, that Smith's having his survey made so far from Thomas' land was to secure a location on the road to Conococheague for the purpose of opening a tavern. The beginning point for SMITHFIELD was "a bounded white oak standing on the south side of the Main Road about 5 perches from the said road."

Smith presented a petition to the Frederick County Court of November 1751[3] in which he stated, "Your petitioner living on a Main Road that leads from Frederick Town to Conocochigue and is desirous to keep a public house of Entertainment, therefore prays your Worships to grant him license for so doing." The Court ordered that "said petitioner have the effect of his Prayer on giving surety according to law."

But almost immediately Smith found himself in trouble with the law. At the March Court of 1752, the Grand Jury made the following presentment: "Richard Smith Innholder for abusing Alexander McDonald who

---

[3] Frederick County Judgment Records, D-160.

called in at his house in Bad Weather."[4] The Court
"Ordered that Richard Smith keep Tavern no longer,
it appearing to the Court here that he is a person of
bad character."[5]

There is inconclusive evidence that Smith may
have had his license restored for a time, but his fortunes steadily declined. He became indebted to Josiah
Beall in 1754 and in the November Court of 1755 confessed judgment to Beall for 2 pounds, 1 shilling,
2 pence and 4,412 pounds of tobacco. In June 1758,
by condemnation, Beall became the owner of SMITH-
FIELD.

On July 8, 1766 for a consideration of 66 pounds,
Josiah Beall sold SMITHFIELD to Michael Jesserong.[6]
Görg Michel Jeserang and his father, Bartholmi Jes-
erang, had arrived in Philadelphia on the ship "Loyal
Judith" on September 3, 1739.[7] In a 1751 deed from
Daniel Dulany to Bartholomew Jesserong, conveying
Lot Nos. 49, 57, 58 and 59 in Fredericktown, Bar-
tholomew Jesserong is described as a "taylor."[8]

So also is Michael Jesserong in a 1759 deed for a
lot in Fredericktown.[9] But in a deed dated March 3,
1767 from Michael Jesserong to Peter Brown for Lot
No. 2 in Middletown, Michael is described as a "tavern
keeper."[10] This gives rise to the speculation that
Michael Jesserong may have operated Smith's inn after
Smith lost SMITHFIELD and that he was a tavern
keeper in Middletown while he was selling lots there.

Between July 8, 1766 and March 3, 1767 Michael

---

[4] Ibid., D-331.

[5] Ibid., D-337.

[6] Frederick County Land Records, K-662.

[7] Ralph B. Strassburger and William J. Hinke,
Pennsylvania German Pioneers (Norristown, Pa.,
1934), vol. 1, pp. 265, 269, 272.

[8] Frederick County Land Records, B-466.

[9] Ibid., F-638.

[10] Ibid., K-956.

Jesserong laid off at least 28 lots on SMITHFIELD, 66 x 330 feet each, and on the latter date began selling numbered lots in the town of Middletown for twenty shillings each. Six deeds bear the date of March 3, 1767, and they conveyed Lot Nos. 2, 4, 7, 14, 24, and 28. Between March 3, 1767 and August 15, 1768 he sold ten more lots: 1, 3, 5, 8, 10, 12, 19, 21, 26 and 27. All lots were subject to a yearly ground rent of 7 shillings, 6 pence — or approximately $1.00 — payable March 3rd of each year to Michael Jesserong. (For a summary of the original sales of lots in Middletown, see below, p. 146.)

And then on August 15, 1768, for reasons unknown, Jesserong sold the entire tract of 44 acres to Conrad Crone for 60 pounds.[11] The deed of transfer doesn't so recite, but it seems obvious that it transferred not only all unsold lots to Crone, but also the ground rents on lots already sold.

This is indicated by the fact that after August 15, 1768 all original sales thus far found of unsold lots are by Crone, with ground rents payable to Crone. Also, with one unexplained exception,[12] all resales of lots first sold by Jesserong provide for payment of ground rents to Crone.

The sale of SMITHFIELD as acreage and not as 12 unsold lots with surrounding unplatted acreage has caused confusion in some quarters — so much so that some have contended that Jesserong's lots were not laid out on SMITHFIELD at all. In order to locate, on SMITHFIELD, as many land transfers as possible, the accompanying plat of SMITHFIELD with explanatory notes had been prepared (see pp. 142-145). Only those lots which could be definitely located have been platted. The platting of these land sales also shows several transactions of some historical interest.

On the same day the 44 acres of SMITHFIELD

---

[11] Ibid., L-397.
[12] Ibid., M-338.

were sold to Crone, Jesserong repurchased from Crone four acres for six pounds,[13] together with Lots 26 and 27 for two shillings each.[14] The ground rents for these two lots were made payable to Crone, and this is still stronger evidence that the sale of the whole tract carried wiht it the transfer of ground rents.

There is no indicated reason for this repurchase by Jesserong, but a 1797 equity suit may furnish at least a partial explanation. This was a suit by Joseph Swearingen's Lessee against Philip Nollert and George Shifeler, involving title to four lots in Middletown (not identified by numbers) which were owned or occupied by the defendants.

On August 15, 1797, in obedience to an order of the General Court of the Western Shore, Samuel Duvall, Surveyor for Frederick County, prepared a plat of WATSON'S WELFARE and SMITHFIELD according to the claims of the parties to the suit. This plat shows WATSON'S WELFARE overlapping the western part of SMITHFIELD and nearly the whole of that tract south of the Main Road.

The western overlap of approximately four acres was not involved in the suit. Obviously Jesserong was aware of his defective title to this acreage and had abandoned claim to it in 1768 at the time he repurchased it from Crone (see Plat and Note A, p. 143). The decision of the Chancery Court in the matter of the four lots is not found.

It is by this time obvious that Middletown was originally platted nine years before the Declaration of Independence, and not by Margaret Crone. Indeed, since Margaret lived to at least 1839, it is also obvious that when Middletown was laid out, she was a small child, or perhaps as yet unborn.

There is nothing in the land records to indicate that Margaret ever owned either any land or any

---

[13] Ibid., L-507.
[14] Ibid., L-506.

ground rents before 1808. Conrad Crone's will was probated November 25, 1808, and therein he devised to his daughter Margaret "my house and all my lotts adjoining Middletown, with all the ground rent of said Middletown."[15]

Margaret Crone died intestate, and the First and Final Account of her Administrator was filed February 16, 1841.[16] In that account accruals of ground rents are shown from March 1, 1839 to December 15, 1839, amounting to $34.32\frac{3}{4}$. Accrual to this latter date may indicate the date of Margaret's death.

Her estate was divided among numerous heirs-in-common, and it is possible that this fragmentation may have brought an end to ground rents in Middletown. None of Margaret's heirs erected a stone to her memory, and she lies in an unmarked grave, as do her father and mother.

SMITHFIELD — 44 ACRES

The following plat is based on courses and distances of the original patent dated October 10, 1750 together with its certificate of survey recorded at the Hall of Records in Annapolis.[17] Land sales have been added in identifiable positions for a dual purpose: (1) There have been doubts expressed by some that the original lots platted and sold by Michael Jesserong were actually on SMITHFIELD. These doubts arise primarily from the sale by Jesserong to Conrad Crone of the entire 44 acres of SMITHFIELD with no mention in the deed of either the previously sold lots or the ground rents thereon. Since the areas platted are all identified or identifiable as being on SMITHFIELD, they effectively remove such doubts. (2) This platting, to the extent it

---

[15] Frederick County Will Record, GMRB 1-425.
[16] Frederick County Administrative Accounts, GME 14-196.
[17] Land Office Patent Record BY & GS 5-616.

is possible, permits comparison with the only known reasonably accurate map of early Middletown, [18] and such comparison is further proof of the location of the original town on SMITHFIELD.

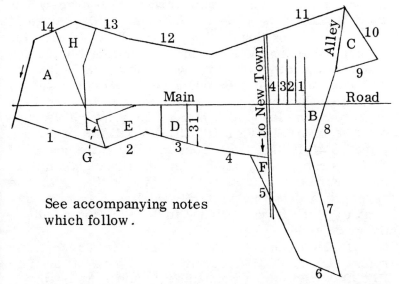

See accompanying notes which follow.

A. This is the 4 acres of SMITHFIELD which Jesserong bought back from Crone simultaneously with his sale of the entire 44 acres. There is no evidence in the land records that Jesserong ever transferred this parcel to anyone. There was a controversial overlap of part of this small acreage with WATSON'S WELFARE, which was claimed by Van Swearingen, who in his 1784 will transferred his title thereto to his son Joseph Swearingen. (See also Note G.)

B. This irregular unnumbered lot passed from Crone to Hennickhousen, October 20, 1787 (WR 7-522). The east side (first line) of this lot, running N21°E 22 with the eighth line of SMITHFIELD is described as extending "to the middle of the Main Road." Its north side (second line) ran N88°W and is apparently down

---

[18] C.O. Titus, <u>Atlas of Frederick County</u> (1873), p.67.

the center of the road "to Lot 10." This location for Lot 10 appears entirely unreasonable, but the not very reliable 1829 plat of Middletown by H. G. O'Neal, Surveyor, shows a Lot 10 at this location and another Lot 10 on the north side of Main Street in sequence westward from Lot 1. (The 1829 plat is found on page 24 of the Frederick County Levy Court Road Record for 1828.) Assuming the road ran in a straight line, given two known points, the course of the road can be laid on.

This middle-of-the-road point is corroborated by Land Record W-583, January 29, 1776, from Peter Jesserong to Jacob Gardner, conveying 56 square perches of RESURVEY ON CHEVY CHASE which adjoined SMITHFIELD on the east. The third course of this deed, beginning at the "end of the eighth line of SMITHFIELD," ran S21°W 14 (which is the eighth line reversed and is that part of said line, 36 perches in length, which is not included in "B") [to the middle of the great road].

C. This unnumbered lot, Crone to Jacob Lawrence (Lorentz), is described as "part of SMITH-FIELD" (WR 9-490, October 29, 1790). Its beginning point is the end of the eighth line of SMITHFIELD, and its three courses are the same as lines 9, 10 and 11 of SMITHFIELD, "to the middle of the alley, then by and with said alley to the beginning." This permits insertion of the alley, but without its known width.

D. Crone to Philip Appleman, tanner. There are two references to this transaction: WR 9-182 (recorded April 15, 1790) and WR 13-620 (dated November 6, 1795). The former, for a consideration of £10, purported to convey Lots 32 and 33. But the latter stated there was an error and it was then executed to correct it. In so doing the tract was described by courses and distances. It is located here because its description places it adjacent to Lot 31, which can then be established. Lots 31, 32 and 33 are obviously not original lots, since all such had a depth of 20 perches. The depth of these three lots varied from 12 to 18 perches, and Lot 31 was given a frontage of 68 feet in partial

144

compensation for its shorter depth. The combined frontage of D (Lots 32 and 33) was about nine perches.

E. Two acres, described as "part of SMITH-FIELD," Crone to Frederick Stemple (WR 16-307, February 13, 1798). The beginning point of E is two perches from the northwest corner of D, which distance is obviously allowance for a street or alley. The third (west) line passes through "the middle of a spring."

F. Crone to Samuel Shoup, James Neale, Thomas Powel, Frederick Stemple, Jr., and Joseph Swearingen, as Trustees, to build "a Seminary of English Learning," for a nominal consideration of $5.00 (WR 27-193, June 29, 1805). This tract began at the end of the fourth line of SMITHFIELD and ran 18 perches with the fifth line "to the road leading to Trap or New Town," which permits location of that road on the plat. However, this road would not have existed in 1767 when Middletown was platted, since New Town (part of Jefferson) was not laid out until 1774.

G & H. These two small parcels represent a reciprocal transaction on September 25, 1820, whereby for a mutual consideration of $2.00, Joseph Swearingen transferred parcel G to Margaret Crone (JS 11-545), and Margaret deeded Swearingen parcel H (JS 11-547). These transactions are of interest only because parcel G was a part of parcel A, and there is no indication in the land records how Swearingen's title thereto was definitely established.

LOTS 1, 2, 3, 4. Placing these lots as shown permits, by measurement, the laying out of 18 additional lots of 66 feet frontage west of the New Town Road, with a $16\frac{1}{2}$ foot alley between each group of four lots and an alley of similar width west of the last lot, which would therefore be Lot 22. It seems rather obvious, therefore, that this was the original plan of the Town, and that the map in Titus' 1873 Atlas is a faithful reproduction of that plan. The western edge of the last lot, Lot 22, would therefore be $16\frac{1}{2}$ feet from the eastern line of the small parcel H.

145

SALE OF ORIGINAL LOTS IN MIDDLETOWN
(Scheduled by the Author)

Liber and Page	Deed Dated	Grantor	Grantee	Consideration	Ground Rent To
			LOT #1		
L-250	3/19/68 ?	Jesserong[1] ?	Margaret Jesserong ?	20s	Jesserong[1]
O-507	8/21/71	Jesserong	Peter Stuck	20s	Jesserong
RP-82	6/ 7/77	Stuck	Crone[2]	£101	By Crone to Owner of town
			LOT #2		
K-956	3/ 3/67	Jesserong	Peter Brown	20s	Jesserong
			LOT #3		
L-248	3/19/68	Jesserong	Magdalena Jesserong	20s	Jesserong
M-441	8/21/69	Magdalena Jesserong	Michael Sturm	£3	Magdalena Jesserong
			LOT #4		
K-997	3/ 3/67	Jesserong	Mathias Brandenburg	20s	Jesserong
P-323	8/18/72	Brandenburg	Harman Yost	£4	Crone[2]
			LOT #5		
L-249	3/19/68	Jesserong	Mary Jesserong	20s	Jesserong
			LOT #6[3]		
O-139	3/20/71	Crone[2]	Luth. Ch. Trustees Valentine Motter, Philip Judy, Sam'l. Bossert	1p	Crone - one pepper grain
			LOT #7		
K-1081	3/ 3/67	Jesserong	Nicholas Helfenstein	20s	Jesserong
L-393	3/15/68	Helfenstein	John Spoon	£5	Jesserong
			LOT #8		
L-74	10/ 9/67	Jesserong	Herman Yost	20s	Jesserong
P-420	11/20/72	Yost	Frederick Stemple	£5	Crone
			LOT #9		
WR 5-385	3/17/84	Crone	Adam Herring	£1	Crone
			LOT #10		
K-1393	6/17/67	Jesserong	Samuel Buzzard	10s	Jesserong
			LOT #11		
WR 8-656	10/10/89	Crone	Jacob Fulwider	20s	Crone
			LOT #12		
L-246	3/19/68	Jesserong	Nicholas Helfenstein	20s	Jesserong
			LOT #13		
WR 2-271	10/16/79	Crone	Abraham Faw	£25	Crone
WR 4-101	6/10/83	Faw	Henry Feaster, Jr.	£30	Crone
WR 6-156	8/29/85	Feaster	George Gephart	£35	Crone
			LOT #14		
K-1055	3/ 3/67	Jesserong	Conrad Crone	20s	Jesserong
WR 2-271	10/16/79	Crone	Abraham Faw	£25	Crone
WR 4-101	6/10/83	Faw	Henry Feaster, Jr.	£30	Crone
WR 6-156	8/29/85	Feaster	George Gephart	£35	Crone

Liber and Page	Deed Dated	Grantor	Grantee	Consideration	Ground Rent To
			LOT #15		
WR 9-659	3/ 8/91	Crone	Christian Dagenhart	£3	Crone
			LOT #16		
WR 14-41	3/ 7/96	Crone	Matthias Timmerly	£8	Crone
			LOT #17		
WR 14-40	3/ 7/96	Crone	Devalt Sampsell	£3	Crone
			LOT #18		
WR 14-40	3/ 7/96	Crone	Devalt Sampsell	£3	Crone
			LOT #19		
K-1362	6/17/67	Jesserong	Henry Hamback	20s	Jesserong
			LOT #20		
WR 24-38	11/12/02	Crone	Joseph Castle	£15	Crone
			LOT #21		
K-1393	6/17/67	Jesserong	Samuel Buzzard	10s	Jesserong
			LOT #22		
			LOT #23		
WR 22-594	5/15/02	Crone	Jacob Lawrence	£5	Crone
			LOT #24		
K-1092	3/ 3/67	Jesserong	Harman Yost	20s	Jesserong
N-71	3/20/70	Yost	Peter Jesserong	£60	Jesserong
W-479	1/29/76	P. Jesserong	Michael Rohr	£100	Proprietor of said town for the time being
			LOT #25		
WR 13-229	4/20/95	Crone	George Marteney		Crone

This deed corrects an earlier unrecorded deed which erroneously conveyed #27.

Liber and Page	Deed Dated	Grantor	Grantee	Consideration	Ground Rent To
			LOT #26		
L-506	8/15/68	Crone	Jesserong	2s	Crone
			LOT #27		
L-245	3/19/68	Jesserong	Daniel Jesserong	20s	Jesserong
	?	?	?		
L-506	8/15/68	Crone	Jesserong	2s	Crone
N-178	6/25/71	Jesserong	George Shifler	£19/10s	Crone
			LOT #28		
K-981	3/ 3/67	Jesserong	Frederick Miller	20s	Jesserong
M-338	6/24/69	Miller	Mich. Sheneberger	£24	Jesserong
WR 7-293	5/ 4/87	Sheneberger	Geo. Shively (cf. Shifler, Lot #27)	£45	Crone
			LOT #29		
WR 8-402	3/13/89	Crone	Henry Beckley	£2/10s	Crone
			LOT #30		
WR 8-402	3/13/89	Crone	Henry Beckley	£2/10s	Crone
			LOT #31		
WR 8-672	10/31/89	Crone	Frederick Stemple	£3	Crone

68 foot front "running back to outlines of SMITHFIELD"

Liber and Page	Deed Dated	Grantor	Grantee	Consideration	Ground Rent To
			LOTS #32-33[4]		
WR 9-182	4/15/90[5]	Crone	Philip Appleman	£5 ea. lot	Crone
WR 13-620	11/ 6/95				
			UNNUMBERED LOT		
N-167	6/25/71	Jesserong	Henry Alexander	£3/15s	Jesserong
			UNNUMBERED LOT		
WR 7-522	10/20/87	Crone	Derrick Hennickhousen	£3	Crone

[1] [George] Michael Jesserong.
[2] Conrad Crone.
[3] On March 30, 1771 (O-139), for a consideration of "one penny sterling," Conrad Crone deeded Lot #6 in Middletown to Valentine Motter, Philip Judy and Samuel Bossert, as trustees to build "finished and completed....one church edifice for publick worship for the use and service of a congregation of Lutheran Augustine Confession....yielding and paying the rent of one pepper grain yearly." Titus' 1873 Atlas shows the Lutheran [sic] Church on Lot #6, and it has apparently occupied that Lot since 1771.
[4] See "D" — pp. 143-144.
[5] Date recorded.

Additional Notes of Historical Interest

On February 13, 1798 (WR 16-305) Conrad Crone conveyed an irregularly shaped lot, said to contain three-quarters of an acre, to the trustees of the Middletown Lutheran Church who at that time were Frederick Stemple, Nicholas Powlas, George Powlas and Peter Haller. The beginning point for this lot was a stone planted "about six feet from the northwest corner of the stone house called 'the Parson's House'." This point would apparently be what is now the southeast corner of Washington and Jefferson Streets, where the old stone house still stands. On March 1, 1848 (WBT 8-470) the trustees of the Lutheran Church sold the "Parson's House" lot to Henry Lighter for $1,350.

On January 20, 1803 (WR 23-647) five citizens of Middletown executed a bond of $1,000 to the state of Maryland to guarantee payments to winners in a lottery they proposed to conduct The five citizens were Frederick Stemple, Thomas Powel, Pator (?) Showman, Henry Stemple and Samuel Shoup. They planned to raise $400 to buy a fire engine "for the safety of Middletown." The outcome of their project is unknown.

WALKERSVILLE — IT JUST GREW

N.B. In 1972 I was asked by the Mayor of
Walkersville, Maryland to prepare, as the
first chapter of a proposed history of the
town, a brief sketch of its beginnings. Since
the historical project has not developed, I include my proposed chapter here.

Present-day Walkersville lies on parts of three
original tracts of land: MONOCACY MANOR, SPRING
GARDEN and DULANY'S LOTT.

MONOCACY MANOR, a tract of about 9,000
acres, was surveyed for Lord Baltimore on May 29,
1724. Its beginning point was the mouth of Glade
Creek at the Monocacy River, and its southern boundary ran N 74° E from there to a point near Daysville.
Its eastern boundary ran approximately north from that
point to intersect an eastern extension of Gravel Hill
Road. That road, not then in existence, would have
been its northern boundary, projected due west to the
Monocacy River. The River then formed its western
boundary.[1]

The Manor was laid off into farms, or lots, which
were numbered. The purpose was to attract German
settlers on these farms by leasing them at nominal
rentals. After the Manor was confiscated as British
property by the State of Maryland in 1781, it was re-

---

[1] Maryland Land Office, Hall of Records, Patent
Records, IL #A-198

surveyed into 85 lots, several of them very small, which were sold at public auction.[2]

On May 28, 1724, 3,850 acres, called DULANY'S LOTT, was surveyed for Daniel Dulany, one of Lord Baltimore's agents. It also had its beginning point at the mouth of Glade Creek, and its northern boundary ran N 84° E from that point to beyond Israel's Creek. Its southern boundary extended below present Maryland Route #26.[3]

These two surveys left between them a V-shaped wedge, ten degrees wide. There are several theories why this ten-degree triangle was left between the MANOR and DULANY'S LOTT, but the most plausible seems to be that it was merely a surveyor's error resulting from a misunderstanding. Whatever the cause, on November 14, 1730 John Abbington, a land speculator, succeeded in having it surveyed for himself. He called it SPRING GARDEN.[4]

It seems obvious that Dulany thought his northern boundary ran N 74° E, contiguous with the southern boundary of the Manor, for on at least one occasion he sold a part of SPRING GARDEN to William Dern. He bought SPRING GARDEN from Abbington on June 9, 1738 for £100.[5] From that time on it was actually a part of DULANY'S LOTT, though it retained its original name of SPRING GARDEN in subsequent land transactions.

In present-day terms the northern boundary of SPRING GARDEN — and hence the southern boundary of MONOCACY MANOR — crosses Fulton Avenue in Walkersville approximately 525 feet south of the north curb of Pennsylvania Avenue. Crum Road, which

---

[2] Maryland Land Office Sale Book of Confiscated British Property, 1781-1785.

[3] Maryland Land Office, Hall of Records, Patent Records, EI5-244.

[4] Ibid., AM1-31.

[5] Prince George's County Land Records, I-597.

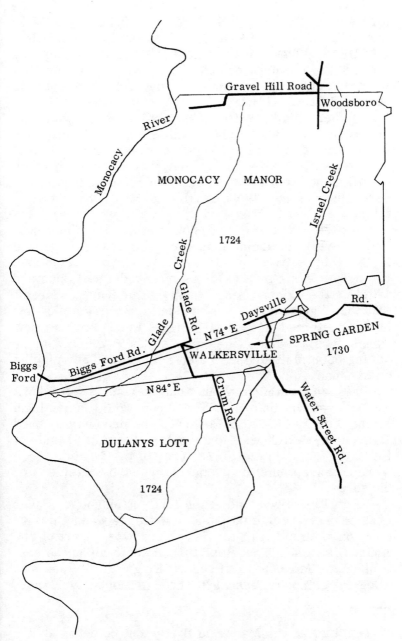

Original Land Surveys Near Walkersville

151

forms a part of the 1967 Corporate Boundary of Walkersville, is on the southern boundary line of SPRING GARDEN. That line, extended westward, passes through the Elementary School Grounds and Glade Village. In spite of its name, Spring Garden Estates is not on SPRING GARDEN.

Modern Walkersville is a combination of two towns — Georgetown and Walkersville — which, until the formation of Walkersville Election District in 1904, were so little a joint entity that they were themselves in different election districts: Georgetown in Woodsboro District and Walkersville in Mt. Pleasant District.

Neither of these towns was platted. They just grew. While it seems most probable that Georgetown is the older settlement, there is no way of determining its age. Varle's 1808 map of Frederick County,[6] which is the oldest reliable map of the county, doesn't show Georgetown. It was evidently a village of a few houses situated along the Biggs Ford Road — now Pennsylvania Avenue in Walkersville — which, never having been platted, Varle also didn't dignify by placing on his map.

It seems rather obvious that no houses were built in Georgetown before 1781. They would have been situated on MONOCACY MANOR, the property of Lord Baltimore, which was for lease as farm land and not for sale. And, in the 1782 survey of the Manor, there were no exceptions for property owned by outside purchasers.

Biggs Ford was one of the earliest Monocacy River crossings. It came into use as a tie between the settlers on both sides of the River and was a part of the Annapolis Road. That Road turned south along the east bank of the Monocacy. Present Biggs Ford Road was a logical extension eastward through Monocacy Manor,

------

[6] Original at the Maryland Historical Society, Baltimore.

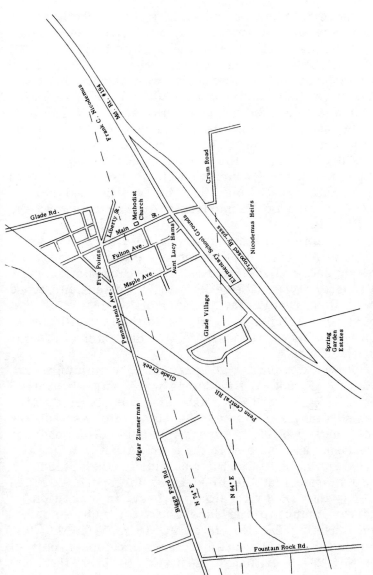

Walkersville and Vicinity

153

and there is a strong probability that, together with Water Street Road and Crum Road, it may have formed later alternate routes for the Annapolis Road.

For some unknown reason, when Biggs Ford Road was laid out, its northern edge was placed on the lot lines of the lots north of it, and therefore its entire width was taken from those lots below it. The universal practice in opening roads was to take half the width of a road from each property along whose boundaries it ran. Hence the northern boundary line of all properties in the Manor south of the Road is the north edge of the Road. And, in Walkersville, all lots on the south side of Pennsylvania Avenue extend to the north curb.

It is not clear whether Biggs Ford Road (or Pennsylvania Avenue) ever extended eastward from its present end at Glade Road or always turned at an angle up Liberty Street at Five Points. Its extension beyond Glade Road would have been most logical, for that would have carried it straight into the Daysville Road. However, by whatever route, it did extend into the Daysville Road.

It was not until the house and outbuildings now owned by Frank C. Nicodemus were built about 1866 that the Biggs Ford Road extension was diverted to the present Maryland Route #194 at a point west of the Nicodemus dwelling. Liberty Street is now a dead-end street ending at a point in the town's limits, a line extended southward from the east side of Glade Road.

Evidence that the Road for a long time extended directly into Daysville Road is found in a petition by Andrew Adams to the June Court of 1768. Adams, then tenanting Lot No. 29 of MONOCACY MANOR (the present Thomas L. Cramer farm occupies a part of Lot No. 29), petitioned the Court to have the road moved closer to his lot line. He said that as it was presently located it cut off a narrow strip between road and line which he found difficult to cultivate. He described the road as "being the road that leads from Biggs Ford on Monocacy Creek, the East side, to

154

Israels Creek and so to Baltimore Town."[7]

As previously noted, the village of Walkersville along what is now Route #194 apparently came into being considerably later than Georgetown. On May 2, 1814 John Walker bought from Nicholas Randall $269\frac{3}{4}$ acres of FEDERAL for $26,975.[8] This acreage was estimated without survey, and no courses and distances are given in the deed.

FEDERAL was patented to Thomas Beatty on January 5, 1790 for 317 acres.[9] It was a resurvey on three lots: No. 75 of MONOCACY MANOR, No. 16 of DULANY'S LOTT, and No. 8 which was primarily SPRING GARDEN but partly DULANY'S LOTT. Its approximate boundaries were as follows: on the east present Crum Road and Main Street, on the north the north curb of Pennsylvania Avenue, on the west the present Edgar Zimmerman farm and extension of the western boundary of the present Nicodemus Heirs' farm, and on the south the approximate boundaries of that same farm. It is emphasized that these boundaries are approximate, for two unidentified small tracts, totaling about 47 acres, had been sold from the original 317 acres of the three lots — approximately 17 acres by Beatty and 30 acres by Randall.

There is nothing evident in the land records to indicate any ownership of dwellings on this land in 1814, but that statement is made with reservations. However, it is obvious that dwellings and a few shops were built within a few years. Bond's 1858 Map of Frederick County[10] shows the Walkersville Post Office and a store in the name of Mrs. R. Biser approximately where Aunt Lucy Hams, Inc., is now located. Farther west, across the street, shops of a cabinet

---

[7] Frederick County Judgment Records, P-178.
[8] Frederick County Land Records, WR 46-515.
[9] Ibid., WR 10-679; Frederick County Survey Records, HGO 1-294.
[10] Copy at Artz Library, Frederick.

155

maker and a pump maker are shown. And dwellings are shown on both sides of the road (present Maryland Route #194). This road was originally designated "the road from Fredericktown to Pennsylvania" and was laid out in the late 1740s on petition by Joseph Wood.[11]

Also shown on Bond's map are several houses in Georgetown, the Methodist Church on the country road which has become Main Street, and several dwellings on that road near Five Points.

In short, these two little villages were beginning to be bound together by settlers along the only road connecting them. Fulton Avenue and Maple Avenue were yet to be opened. But the two villages were moving toward union under the name of Walkersville if for no other reasons than that Walkersville had a post office and Georgetown did not: Residents of the latter were being addressed by their correspondents as living at Walkersville.

Formal union came in 1892 when the two settlements were incorporated as Walkersville and a town government, consisting of a Burgess and Commissioners, was set up.

---

[11] Frederick County Judgment Records (March Court, 1748), A-18.

THREE LOST TOWNS

The first sixteen pages of the following are a part, somewhat revised and foreshortened, of a paper I read before the Frederick County Historical Society on April 20, 1971. My principal purpose in presenting the paper was to refute the claim which, like Banquo's ghost, arises periodically in the Frederick community concerning the existence of a very early town of Monocacy.

Mr. John P. Dern has collaborated in the discussion, beginning on page 173, of the probable location of the first Lutheran Church, built in 1743, which the proponents of the mythical town of Monocacy always assume was in that town.

The towns of Hamburgh and Trammelstown were added for their own mild interest and to justify the title.

* * * *

Of the three towns with which this discussion is concerned, one was swallowed up by leviathan, one was still-born, and one, in my opinion, was never conceived.

HAMBURGH

The first of these towns is Hamburgh. From time to time I have asked friends if they knew where it was located. In all cases, except those who disclaimed any knowledge whatever of the town, they have located

157

it on top of Catoctin Mountain at the Hamburg fire tower. It is true that for many years there have been several houses in that general location. But there was never a platted town.

Actually the town of Hamburgh, while it apparently bordered Frederick County, was in Prince George's County and is now embodied in the city of Washington, D.C.[1] Its primary interest to Frederick Countians lies in the fact that a number of its people bought lots in Hamburgh.

In 1768 Jacob Funk, who had owned land in Frederick County since 1753, laid out the town of Hamburgh on a tract he owned just over the Frederick County line in Prince George's County. Apparently it adjoined Georgetown, D. C., which was then in Frederick County.

Strangely enough, Funk filed a plat of Hamburgh in Prince George's County Land Records. It showed 287 lots, but for reasons unknown 53 of these were not offered for sale. Nor is there any indication of the total number of lots, at £5 each, which were sold.

I remark about Funk's filing of his plat because few planners of towns, at least in Frederick County, did so. Moreover, in the same year that Funk was promoting Hamburgh, he was also promoting Jerusalemtown, which was then in Frederick County, but which we now know as Funkstown in Washington County. He didn't file a plat of Jerusalemtown in the Frederick County Land Records.

The early Kemp brothers, Christian and Gilbert,

---

[1] If this statement appears somewhat cryptic, it should be remembered that Frederick County, when it was formed in 1748 out of Prince George's County, included today's Montgomery County and half of today's District of Columbia. See, for example, frontispiece map in Gaius Marcus Brumbaugh, Maryland Records, Colonial, Revolutionary, County and Church from Original Sources (Baltimore, 1915), vol. 1.

each owned two lots in Hamburgh. In his will, probated in 1790, Christian Kemp wrote, "I give to my....
sons Daniel and David my two lots (Nos. 11 & 178)....
in the Town called Hamburg on Potowmack River which
I bought from Jacob Funk."[2]   And when Gilbert Kemp
made his will in June 1791, he devised Lot No. 109 "in
Hamburgh Town" to his daughter Catherine Houx [wife
of John Houck, Sr.] and Lot No. 221 to his daughter
Barbara [wife of John] Brunner.[3]

In October 1790 President Washington selected the
site for the "Federal City," or the national capital,
which was named Washington in his honor. He persuaded those owning land within the new city's boundaries to sell their holdings to the Government for £25
per acre, or approximately $66, the pound then being
worth about $2.67.   I have not been able to learn from
Prince George's County Records what Funk received
for the unsold portion of Hamburgh.

W. B. Bryan has noted that Funk's tract "extended
from a short distance west of what is now 19th Street
NW to west of 23rd Street and from H Street to the
River...."[4] A portion of George Washington University
is therefore situated on the northern part of Hamburgh.

And so Hamburgh was swallowed by Leviathan!

TRAMMELSTOWN

In my opinion, Trammelstown — sometimes also
known as Trammelsburg — never existed as a platted
town. It is true that at and near the intersection of
Maryland Route #464 and the County Road from Point
of Rocks to Frederick, where the Point of Rocks Episcopal Church now stands, a few houses once were
grouped and called Trammelstown. But that was not

---

[2]   Frederick County Will Records, GM 2-330.
[3]   Ibid., GM 2-516/517.
[4]   W. B. Bryan, A History of the National Capital
(New York, 1914), vol. 1, p. 59.

the town John Trammel envisioned in his 1784 will.

In that will Trammel directed his executors, who were his daughter Sarah Trammel DeLashmutt and her husband Lindsey DeLashmutt, to lay out 400 lots for a town. The lots were to be 60 x 120 feet in size, "with suitable and convenient streets and alleys." Half of the lots were devised to Sarah Trammel DeLashmutt and half to Sarah's son, Trammel DeLashmutt.

The 400 lots were to be laid off, said John Trammel, "On that part of my lands called TRAMMEL'S CONOY ISLANDS and WOODLAND which lies between SWEDES FOLLY and Potowmack River." The lots were to be sold "for 8 silver dollars...." with yearly ground rent of "not less than 18 shillings [then about $2.40]."[5]

SWEDES FOLLY lay about one mile, approximately north-northwest, from present-day Point of Rocks and had been owned by the Nelson and DeLashmutt families for at least forty years prior to 1784.

I have searched the Land Records carefully, but I can find no record of lot sales by either Trammel DeLashmutt or his mother. Lindsey Delashmutt died in October or November of 1791. Shortly thereafter, in the following March — and that may have caused some raised eyebrows — Sarah married Ralph Briscoe. She devised "the lands my father gave me" to the two sons she had by DeLashmutt but in so doing nowhere made any mention of town lots.[6]

Trammel DeLashmutt died in 1810 and during his lifetime was involved in numerous purchases and sales of land, some of which apparently included the lands his grandfather had given him and on which Trammelstown was to have been laid out. But there is no mention of town lots in any of them.

There is one transaction in which Trammel DeLashmutt sold to his brother John for $55 "one negro

----

[5] Frederick County Will Records, GM 2-53.
[6] Ibid., GM 3-564.

woman now in the house of said John DeLashmutt in
Trammelsburg." It may have been that Trammelsburg equated with Trammelstown, but it was not the
kind of town John Trammel had in mind when he made
his will in 1784. That town was still-born.

Scharf says briefly of the town that "it was par-
tially destroyed by fire."[7] I suspect a house may have
burned down.

THE TOWN CALLED MONOCACY

At the beginning of this discussion I said that one
of the three lost towns had, in my opinion, never been
conceived. I referred, of course, to the town of
"Monocacy." Actually, so far as I can determine, it
was conceived some 160 years after its assumed birth
— which is something of a miracle.

Its parent was Edward T. Schultz, who in 1896
read before the Frederick County Historical Society a
paper in which he started with the assumption that
there had been such a town and then undertook to find
proof for his hypothesis.[8] In my opinion, his assumption is without foundation and his proof is unconvincing.

In large measure Schultz based his proof on testi-
mony gathered by the Rev. George A. Whitmore of
Thurmont under whose charge the Reformed congregation at Creagerstown was then placed. Together,
these men advanced the conclusion that an "old church"
was located just south of today's Creagerstown, which
Schultz then sketched onto a crude map as the site "of
the ancient village of Monocacy."

Whitmore's basis was a series of interviews with
some of the older citizens of Creagerstown concerning

---

[7] J. Thomas Scharf, History of Western Maryland
(Philadelphia, 1882), vol. 1, p. 568.
[8] Edward T. Schultz, "First Settlements of Germans
in Maryland" (Frederick, Md., D. H. Smith, 1896).
Copy in Maryland Historical Society.

the existence of that old log church. He was thus relying almost solely on human memory. But analysis of the ages of his witnesses shows that their memory could have extended no further back in time than to a decade or two at most before the construction in 1834 of the brick church in Creagerstown. [9]

That leaves over 70 years during which any number of old log churches could have been built anywhere in Frederick County, to say nothing of the question how such an observation tied this particular church to a village called "Monocacy."

But, like Parson Weems' cherry-tree story about George Washington, Schultz had "started something." That something snowballed when in 1910 Thomas Williams in his History of Frederick County picked up Schultz's theory and devoted considerable space to almost verbatim quotation of Schultz — even to some of his errors. [10] When the Town-of-Monocacy idea thus became forever embalmed between the hard covers of a history book, it ceased to be an assumption and became instead an accepted fact.

In 1914 Dr. D. W. Nead published a book treating with the early German settlement in Frederick County. There is no clear indication whether he borrowed from Schultz and Williams or arrived at his conclusions independently, but in his book he refers to the First Lutheran Church as "the little log church at the village of Monocacy about 1730."[11]

---

[9] His "oldest and most reliable citizens" were listed as W. L. Grimes, Sr., age 90 (undoubtedly Warner T. Grimes, Sr., 1806-1896, who is buried in Thurmont), and two ladies "bordering on 80 years," namely Mrs. Michael Zimmerman (1814-1904 of Creagerstown) and Miss Melisia Myers (Mrs. Melissa C. Myers, 1825-1904, also of Creagerstown).

[10] T. J. C. Williams and Folger McKinsey, History of Frederick County, Maryland (Hagerstown, 1910), pp. 2-5.

162

Following the publication of the Williams History and because of its wider local circulation, speculation began to develop concerning the location of Monocacy Town. Within the past three or four decades that speculation has intensified. Various theories, based on old cemeteries and ancient foundations, have been put forward and defended.

As I understand them, these theories, while differing widely as to location of "Monocacy Village," have one thing in common, namely that they all associate their "village" closely with the first, or Monocacy, Lutheran Church. They all assume that that church was in their village. I do not intend to become involved more than superficially in those theories except to say that I think a careful search of Frederick County Land Records will establish private ownership of these suspected town sites which will rather effectively eliminate them as such.

In 1941 Folger McKinsey, "The Bentztown Bard," former city editor of the Frederick News, member of the staff of the Baltimore Sun and co-author of the History of Frederick County,[12] wrote a series of articles for the Sun[13] in which he repeated the Schultz-inspired belief that the town of Monocacy was located at the point where Hunting Creek empties into the Monocacy River near Creagerstown.

"This town of Monocacy," he wrote, "Must have been considerable of a town in its day, for it is frequently mentioned in historical letters and records and was quite well known to people engaged in the settling of the Maryland-Pennsylvania borders."

Schultz's map was reprinted in 1950 in the local Frederick newspaper. "Way back in the early 1700's," the accompanying article read, "The little village of

---

[11] Daniel W. Nead, The Pennsylvania German in the Settlement of Maryland (Lancaster, Pa., 1914), p. 93.
[12] Williams and McKinsey, op. cit.
[13] Baltimore Sun, July 7, 8, 9, 1941.

Monocacy was the hub of the county (Frederick had not yet been settled) and the old Monocacy road — long since extinct — was the major thoroughfare of its day."[14] Quite obviously, this essay was little more than another rehash of Schultz's paper.

Some forty years ago a small stone was set up along the old Woodsboro-Creagerstown Road about three-quarters of a mile south of Creagerstown. Based on "research" (which is no longer available) by the then Reformed pastor Peter E. Heimer, the stone bore the inscription, "Site of Old Monocacy Log Church Built 1732." Ignoring its errors both in time and location, we can but decry the indelible impressions left by such "authoritative" stone monuments. Their authenticity is as little questioned as popular "history" books.

Dr. Grace Tracey[15] has solidly refuted Schultz's claim that Creagerstown is the site of both early village and church. From her work with the old land records, she observed that until the year 1759 only three persons, not one of them a German or a Lutheran, owned property between today's Creagerstown and the Monocacy River. Moreover, on only one of the three parcels was there at the time of survey so much as a single log house of 20 x 16 foot dimensions; on the other tracts there were no structures whatsoever.[16]

---

[14] Frederick News, January 27, 1950. It was not until 1748 that the area of today's Frederick County, together with that of all the three later counties west of it, was created from Prince George's County as a separate county. The term "hub of the county" would thus appear to be a slight overstatement.

[15] Of Hampstead, Maryland. She and her father, Dr. Arthur G. Tracey, spent their respective avocational lifetimes investigating early patents, surveys and deeds pertaining to western Maryland.

[16] For tax purposes the law required that a notation be made on each certificate of survey to describe every

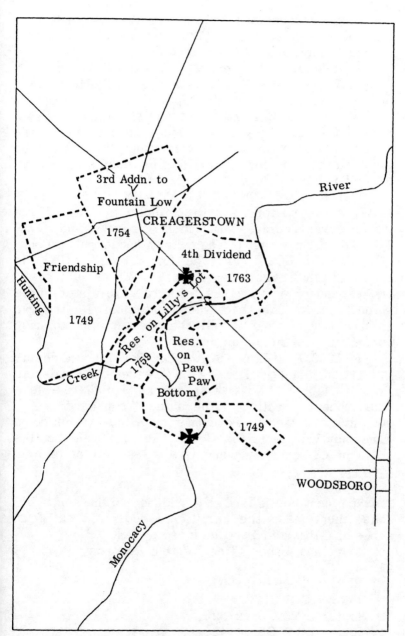

First Patents Near Creagerstown

This hardly describes a village or the possibility of a log church as early as 1732, let alone 1743, even amongst surrounding German farms.

For the record, these were the three tracts:

1) PAW PAW BOTTOM, surveyed initially in 1741 and resurveyed in 1749 for Captain Nathaniel Wickham of the Church of England.[17] It was situated on the east side of the Monocacy River, but extended across the River to include the mouth of Hunting Creek. It also included the crossing of the River by today's Creagerstown-Woodsboro Road.

2) THIRD ADDITION TO RESURVEY ON FOUNTAIN LOW, surveyed for Reverdy Ghiselin in 1754.[18] On its 710 acres Thomas Beatty in 1786 resurveyed TOWN TRACT,[19] on which Creagerstown had been laid out.

3) LILLY'S LOT, surveyed for Richard Lilly, an English Catholic from Conewago, in 1759 as 50 acres[20] and expanded to 300 acres by a resurvey later in the same year.[21] This tract was situated between the two earlier tracts, and it was the one with the notation concerning the single log house.

In 1953 Dr. James Alexander Boyd, then a chemist stationed at Fort Detrick, addressed the Frederick Rotary Club.[22] "That two centuries ago there was a real Monocacy Village," he said, "Is a hard, well-authenticated fact." Boyd then undertook to pin down Monocacy Village in the Ceresville area, eight miles south of Creagerstown and five miles east of today's

---

improvement on the land. In addition to the single log house mentioned, the certificate adds, "About four acres of Cultivated Land Inclosed by fence."

[17] Maryland Land Office, Patent Records, BC & GS 41-15.
[18] Ibid., BC & GS 5-70.
[19] Ibid., IC B-674.
[20] Ibid., BC & GS 12-520.
[21] Ibid., BC & GS 14-42.
[22] Frederick News, May 28, 1953.

downtown Frederick. By "retranslating" some of the early German records, Boyd concluded that Monocacy Village was much nearer to Frederick than Schultz and the others had contended.

Boyd claimed to have remapped the route taken by Pastor Henry Muhlenberg on his visit to Frederick in 1747 and found distances traveled equalled within a mile those of Highway #71.[23] Such calculations are the more remarkable when it is realized that Muhlenberg's reference to "zehen Meilen" (German: ten miles) was translated by Boyd as "three miles."[24]

Boyd also claimed Muhlenberg reported that he returned "several times" from Frederick to night lodgings in Monocacy and concluded the good pastor in so doing and in spite of what he wrote would have traveled three miles but not ten.[25]

When John Derr found outlines of an older stone masonry house in his home on "Dearbought" across the River from Ceresville, Boyd concluded that this might be the very inn where Muhlenberg stayed.[26]

---

[23] Highway #71 has since been renumbered as Maryland Route #194.

[24] Actually Muhlenberg left two versions concerning this distance. In his own record he wrote "einigen" Meilen" (several miles), but in the copy he sent to the authorities in Halle he measured this as "zehen Meilen" (ten miles). (Theodore G. Tappert and John W. Doberstein, The Journals of Henry Melchior Muhlenberg, Philadelphia, 1942, vol. 1, p. 158.) Boyd had translated one or the other as "slightly more than one" and then assumed Muhlenberg was referring — as he actually did no where else — to a "German" mile, equivalent to three (correct: 4.6) "English" miles. In a later passage Muhlenberg quoted the "ten miles" in both versions! See also below, p. 177.

[25] Actually Muhlenberg made one trip to Frederick and so returned only once to his lodgings "in Monocacy,"

[26] Frederick News, loc. cit., May 28, 1953.

Boyd visited the well-known old burying ground on the farm now owned by Ralph Grossnickle along the Monocacy River, north of Ceresville. He claimed evidence of fifty graves — a rather high count by my estimate — and hoped to identify the site as the old Monocacy Village graveyard.[27]

A look at the Land Records shows that the Ceresville cemetery was the property of the Dulanys until 1781, being a part of DULANY'S LOTT granted to Daniel Dulany by Lord Baltimore in 1724. When Tory property was confiscated by the State of Maryland, the cemetery, then designated as Lot No. 18 of DULANY'S LOTT, was sold at the auction held on October 10, 1781. It was bought by William Beatty, grandson of the early Susannah Beatty who had bought from Daniel Dulany, Sr., in 1732 for £200 a 1000-acre part of DULANY'S LOTT to which she brought her family from New York.[28]

William Beatty's purchase was a most logical one, for without doubt a number of the Beatty dead were already buried there. Perhaps the redoubtable Susannah herself was the first occupant of the now-vandalized vault, which may still be seen today.

Dulany's relationships with the aristocratic Beatty clan were doubtless quite close. The other settlers — owners and tenants — on DULANY'S LOTT, together with the numerous Beatty descendants and in-laws, constituted a sizable community of landholders — but by no means a town, as perusal of the Land Records clearly indicates.

There were, for instance, the Biggs, the Far-

---

[27] Jacob M. Holdcraft one year earlier could find only four inscriptions. The recognized thoroughness of Holdcraft's work needs no embellishment from me. See his Names in Stone, 75,000 Cemetery Inscriptions from Frederick County, Maryland (Ann Arbor, 1966), vol. 1, p. 19.

[28] Prince George's County Land Records, Q-532.

quhars, the Ramsburgs, the Derns, all with sizable families, situated along the northern part of DULANY'S LOTT. When deaths began to occur, what more natural than for Dulany to permit them a nearby burial place? It was his land to do with as he pleased. And these people were, in a strong sense, his people. He pleased, therefore, to select an easily accessible, well-drained plot along what was then the principal north-south road on the east bank of the Monocacy. But because the plot remained Dulany's property, it was confiscated and sold in 1781.

Much the same thing had occurred just to the north of present-day Walkersville on MONOCACY MANOR. When, about 1750, the German settlers on and near the MANOR sought a place to build a church and bury their dead, Dulany or Benjamin Tasker, acting as Lord Baltimore's agent, set aside a plot for them. They built a church and buried their dead there. But in 1781, when the MANOR was also confiscated, there was a sizable congregation to object to the sale of that plot. They had no legal title to it, but they appealed to the authorities and, early in 1782 by special act of the Legislature, the "members of the German Reformed Church" were given in fee five acres of land.[29] The Church was later, in 1896, moved into the town of Walkersville, but the original five acres remain in use today as the Glade Cemetery.

And so, with all due respect to Dr. Boyd's research, I cannot agree with his conclusion about the location of an early town at Ceresville, let alone his belief that it was named Monocacy.

The root of the problem in much of this discussion is the mistaken belief that the word "Monocacy" had to refer to a specific town or village. It is perhaps difficult for some modern minds to visualize a countryside completely devoid of towns or villages. And yet that was quite naturally the situation as the first early set-

---

[29] Chapter 8, 1781 Acts of Maryland Legislature.

tlers arrived in what is today Frederick County to lay claim to the virgin land and to divide it into farms of given acreages. Until there were settlers, there was no need for towns or villages.

The earliest land owners were English land speculators, who began acquiring land in the 1720s. They never lived on their lands, but undertook to sell or lease them to others, principally German immigrants. The Germans, for the most part, were farmers seeking land. There were, of course, artisans among them — weavers, tailors, shoemakers, blacksmiths and wheelwrights. But those who plied such trades did so in their homes on a part-time basis for the simple reason that there were not enough people in the area using such services to make them profitable on a fulltime basis. Their principal source of livelihood was farming. They had, therefore, no cause to congregate in a town, and so towns simply did not exist.

There was need, however, to refer to the collective area of these farms as a whole. Yet, without villages or even political subdivisions, the only means of identifying the area lay in associating it with a recognized natural feature. Since the early inhabitants had settled in the valley of the Monocacy River, it was only natural that the word "Monocacy" came to refer to the region as a whole.

Proof of this lies in the geographical distribution of people who called themselves "from Monocacy." Their dispersal argues against the possibility that the word "Monocacy" could refer to any one given locale. Let me recapitulate:

In 1726 Quakers who had settled in the valley received permission from the New Garden Monthly Meeting "to hold religious services on first days [Sundays] in the home of Josiah Ballenger, the Meeting to be called 'Monoquesey'." Ballenger lived in the vicinity of Buckeystown.[30]

------

[30] See above, p. 6.

In 1732 Charles Carroll described a visit to the Susquehanna area of Pennsylvania with John Ross of Annapolis and with John Tredane. Justice Wright of Pennsylvania had a warrant for the arrest of the latter, who was described as "John Tredane of the Province of Maryland, resident of Monochasie."[31] Tredane lived in the area of present-day Union Bridge.[32]

In the same year Joseph Hedges wrote his will, describing himself as "of Manaquicy" in Prince George's County. His land HEDGE HOGG was situated just northwest of Biggs Ford, "lying up Manaquicy Creek on the west side of said creek."[33]

The pioneering Susannah Beatty[34] made her will on June 20, 1742. In it she styled herself as "I, Susannah Beatty of Monocksey."[35] She lived, however, just west of present-day Mount Pleasant on the land now owned by the Glade Valley Farms.

Cornelius Carmack in his 1746 will described himself as "of Monocksey."[36] But he lived near today's Libertytown.[37]

Likewise, Samuel DuVal, who lived in Frederick Town, wrote in his will of 1753 that he was from "Monockezy."[38]

Frederick Unseld, whose home was on BEAUTY near Frederick,[39] wrote his will from "Monksey."[40]

Arnold Livers had his farm in the forks of Owen's

---

[31] John Gibson, History of York County, Pennsylvania (Chicago, 1886), p. 49.
[32] Maryland Land Office, Patent Records, AM 1-54.
[33] Prince George's County Will Records, 20-468.
[34] Cf. above, p. 168.
[35] Frederick County Will Records, A 1-12.
[36] Ibid., A 1-27.
[37] Prince George's County Land Records, Y-571.
[38] Frederick County Will Records, A 1-79.
[39] Maryland Land Office, Patent Records, Y & S 7-115.
[40] Frederick County Will Records, A 1-102.

Creek near present-day Thurmont, but was described to the Maryland Assembly in 1747 as being "at Monocacy."[41]

And, most significantly, an agreement was made on March 28, 1746 between the Reverend Joseph Jennings, "clerk [cleric] rector of All Saints [Church of England] Parish in Monocksesy," and Robert DeButts and Kennedy Farrell.[42]

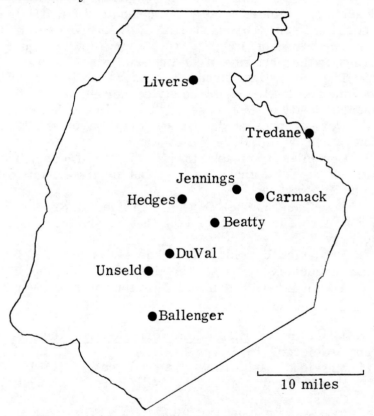

Livers

Tredane

Jennings

Hedges ● ●Carmack

● Beatty

●DuVal

Unseld●

●Ballenger

10 miles

The fact that early settlers, living in such widely scattered localities as Mount Pleasant, Buckeystown,

---

[41]   Maryland <u>Archives</u>, 44-692.
[42]   Prince George's County Land Records, B-14.

Union Bridge, Libertytown, Thurmont and Frederick Town, could designate themselves as "of Monocacy" — whatever its spelling — is the strongest sort of evidence that they were not referring to any single Monocacy town or village. They were referring instead to a general area. And on such evidence I rest my conclusion that the "Town of Monocacy" never existed.

We are left, however, with the question concerning the location of the first Lutheran church in the Monocacy area. Even if it could not exist in what our modern minds think of as a village or town, it did, being central to many of the Germans in the Monocacy Valley, actually exist. The Journal of Pastor Henry Muhlenberg and the church book entries of Pastor Gabriel Näsman attest to that.

From their records we know that the church was of wood construction and was erected in 1743[43] during the short-lived pastorate of David Candler. While he and his flock were Lutherans, the church was also made available to the nearby Reformed settlers.

Before Pastor Candler, there had been no resident pastor in the Monocacy Valley who could minister to the Germans on a full-time basis. Pastor Johann Caspar Stöver, however, did make several trips through the region enroute from his base in Pennsylvania to other German settlements in Virginia. These trips occurred almost every year from 1733 to 1742. He obviously stayed in the homes of the settlers themselves and there conducted services and performed baptisms and marriages for friends and neighbors.

A record of these ministerial acts was kept in his own record book which he presumably carried with him in his saddle bag.[44] From the names of the settlers

---

[43] Boyd (cf. above, p. 166) claimed a "union chapel" was built in "Monocacy Village" about 1728. This date was well before the first land grants to any German settlers.

[44] The original, located in the Historical Society of

found among its entries and the knowledge of their landholdings provided by the work of the Traceys, [45] we can develop a pattern of the German settlement. Very roughly, it extended southward from the Thurmont-Graceham area to TASKER'S CHANCE (on which Frederick was later laid out) and the area to its west.

Stöver is credited with organizing the German Lutherans into a congregation. This he probably did during his more extended visit in November of 1738.[46] But actual construction of the church building itself took place in 1743 under the direction of Pastor Candler, who two years earlier began visiting the Monocacy region from his home at Conewago, near today's Hanover, Pennsylvania. Quite obviously Candler intended to reside permanently in the Monocacy area, for in April 1743 he had surveyed for himself 100 acres of SWINGABACK, just north of today's Bethel.[47] Unfortunately, however, he died at Conewago in late 1744 or early 1745.

After his death a schism with many attendant hard feelings developed among the Monocacy Lutherans. Parishioners who attended Pastor Candler's funeral at Conewago sought the help of Laurentius Nyberg, the Lutheran Pastor at Lancaster who obviously had Herrnhuter leanings. With the help of the Moravians in Bethlehem, he secured for the Monocacy Germans as

---

Pennsylvania, was transcribed by Franklin J. F. Schantz, Rev. John Casper Stoever's Record of Baptisms and Marriages from 1730 to 1779 (Harrisburg, 1896). But the work was so badly anglicized and so poorly proofread that John P. Dern of Redwood City, California has now undertaken a new transcription.

[45] See above, note 15.

[46] Abdel Ross Wentz, The Evangelical Lutheran Church in Frederick, Maryland (Harrisburg, Penna., 1938), p. 53.

[47] Maryland Land Office, Hall of Records, Patent Records, LG E-211.

schoolmaster and precentor one Johann Heinrich Herzer. The following year the Moravian Georg Ninke, an ordained minister, was sent to Monocacy, but the more orthodox Lutherans closed the church to him after only one service. This forced Ninke to meet at Jacob Weller's home for church and school,[48] while the "true" Lutherans turned to Carl Rudolph, an itinerant interloper of questionable morals, who soon deserted them.

Finally an appeal was made to Pastor Muhlenberg, who had arrived in Pennsylvania in 1742. He encouraged Gabriel Näsman, Pastor at Wicaco in Philadelphia, to visit the Monocacy Lutherans in October of 1746 and then came himself in the following June. Just one month earlier the Reformed minister Michael Schlatter, who had arrived in Pennsylvania the year before, also visited Monocacy.

From the accounts left us concerning these various events, we can find three geographical references to the old Monocacy church. Taken together, they reinforce the earlier conclusions reached by Dr. Abdel Ross Wentz and Dr. Arthur Tracey[49] that the actual location was south of today's Thurmont, somewhere near the Jimtown crossroads intersection of Moser Road, Jimtown Road (Maryland Route #550) and Hessong Bridge Road.

It has been a further guess, slightly more precise if not more accurate, that the church stood somewhat south of the Jimtown crossroads, perhaps in the vicinity of Hunting Creek. (See map, p. 180.)

Being unsure of the exact routes of travel taken by the early pastors, I exclude the observation that Pas-

---

[48] In the following year (1747) Jacob Weller and Jacob Matthias sought the help of Dulany in obtaining a warrant for ten acres for church and school. Called DULANY'S GIFT, this marked the beginning of the Moravian congregation and community at Graceham.

[49] See below, p. 182.

tor Muhlenberg in 1747[50] reported traveling 36 miles between the church in Conewago and the homes of his hosts in Monocacy. Pastor Stöver may have traveled the same distance.[51] But using today's roads, I calculate a not too dissimilar distance of at least 32 miles to the Jimtown crossroads.[52]

In the company of two men from Monocacy Muhlenberg left Conewago at two in the afternoon on June 23, 1747, but in a heavy downpour of rain managed before darkness engulfed them to travel only 18 miles. In that distance he saw no houses where they could lodge the night. They continued on another 18 miles, their horses wading knee-deep in water, and finally at two the next morning, half dead and very tired, reached their lodging.

"Nun war ich in der Gegend Manaquesy," wrote

[50] Muhlenberg Journals, op. cit., vol. 1, p. 156. See also Wentz, op. cit., p. 82; and Hallesche Nachrichten von den vereinigten Deutschen Evangelisch-Lutherischen Gemeinen in Nord America, absonderlich in Pensylvanien, Mann, Schmucker and Germann edition (Allentown, 1886), vol. 1, p. 352.

[51] Wentz, op. cit., p. 37, although probably surmised by him from his knowledge of the above Muhlenberg notation.

[52] Undoubtedly Boyd (see above, p. 167) took the 36 miles quite literally and thus placed the Monocacy locale farther south at Ceresville. But the Moravian missionary Leonhard Schnell in his account of a trip in 1743, also from "Canawage," to a crossing of the "Manakes" River near Ceresville marked that distance as 40 miles, an identical difference of four miles. Cf. William J. Hinke and Charles E. Kemper, "Moravian Diaries of Travels Through Virginia," Virginia Magazine of History and Biography, vol. 11 (1904), p. 372. The Ceresville crossing is identified by our knowledge of the location of the land of Abraham Müller, whom Schnell names in his text.

Muhlenberg: "Now I was in the Manaquesy region."[53]

On June 24th Muhlenberg held services which were also attended by three or four of those with Moravian leanings. He called for the church book and wrote in its early pages in English a series of church articles which were then signed by all but the Moravians. The first of these articles claimed the church was built by the Lutherans but was also to be available to the Reformed.[54]

In his account of the following day's activities Muhlenberg gives us the first clue we are seeking:[55] "On June 25th we rode ten miles farther on to a newly laid out town, where several Lutherans lived who belonged to the congregation and could not come hither on the previous day because of the heavy rain."[56]

The new town was, of course, Frederick, and the

---

[53] Muhlenberg Journals, op. cit., (vol. 1, p. 156); Hallesche Nachrichten, op. cit., (vol. 1, p. 352). My underline.

[54] Hallesche Nachrichten, op. cit., p. 353. The entry in the Lutheran Church Book whose original is at the Abdel Ross Wentz Library, Gettysburg Theological Seminary, reads: "The church we have erected and built at Manakasy and used hitherto shall stand and remain and be for the worship of our Protestant Lutheran Religion according to our confession and oeconomie as long the blessed Acts of Tolerance and of our Liberty stand forever, and the reformed congregation shall have liberty for their lawful minister."

[55] See also discussion above, p. 167.

[56] Hallesche Nachrichten, op. cit., p. 355: "Den 25 Junii ritten wir zehen Meilen weiter hinauf zu einer neu angelegten Stadt, wo verschiedene Lutheraner wohneten, wleche mit zu der Gemeine gehören und am vorigen Tage wegen des starken Regens nicht herbei kommen können." For the alternate version, see Muhlenberg Journals, op. cit., vol. 1, p. 158; cf. also above, p. 167, note 24.

distance of "ten miles" gives us an approximate circumference on which to locate the Monocacy Church. The distance was reaffirmed after Muhlenberg related the day's activities: "In the evening we rode the ten miles back again to our former lodging, where several had assembled whom I edified with prayer and song."[57]

The Germans living near Jimtown crossroads were ten miles from Frederick, although the distance to Creagerstown is also ten miles from Frederick. But Ceresville lies less than four miles away.

Small and new though Frederick Town was in 1747, it was a town, whereas the Monocacy Church locale was not. Note Muhlenberg's further comment: "Both groups, in the town and in the country, requested that I might take to heart and lay before our reverend fathers their dispersion, their poverty and their need for a teacher."[58]

The second geographical reference to the Monocacy church may be found in a history of the Graceham Moravian Church written in 1790.[59] The account describes the death of Pastor Candler and the ensuing schism between Lutherans and Moravians as related above. It then gives us the clue for which we have been looking:

"Thereupon Bro. Nyberg communicated with Beth-

---

[57] Ibid. "Am Abend ritten wir die zehen Meilen wieder zurück in unser voriges Quartier, allwo sich einige versammelt, mit welchen mich durch Gebet und Gesang erbauete."
[58] Ibid., p. 355. My underline. Cf. also Muhlenberg Journals, op. cit., vol. 1, p. 158.
[59] Entitled "Historical account of the beginning, progress of the work of the Lord among souls in the neighborhood of the Manacusey in Maryland, and of the gathering and planting of the little congregation of Graceham, associated with the Congregation of the Brethren," this document was found in manuscript form by George Zacharias at the Lititz Archives.

lehem, and on his advice our late sainted Bro. Johann Heinrich Herzer was installed the same year by Bro. Nyberg in the Union Lutheran and Reformed Church then standing two miles from here as their preceptor and schoolmaster, which office he fulfilled faithfully and with blessing until the middle of the year 1746, when an ordained minister, George Nieke, was sent by the Congregation to service the people here,[60] with the gospel and in the school."

"Here," of course, refers to Graceham. From it by road the Creagerstown site is four, not two, miles distant. The mouth of Hunting Creek is nearly five miles away. Ceresville is 11 miles. But it is just a trifle less than two miles to the Jimtown crossroads. And, at the risk of being overly precise, a full two miles would place us slightly south of the crossroads.

Finally, we find an even closer reference from a lengthy entry in the original Lutheran Church Book, the same book in which Pastor Muhlenberg later, but on earlier pages, wrote his articles.[61]

The entry was a copy of a now missing document which had been written in Friederichs Tawn by Pastor Näsman during his visit on October 31, 1746.[62] He took the original document, signed by the congregation's members, with him to the United Ministerium in Pennsylvania. But he wanted to leave a record with the congregation and so made this copy in the local Church Book.

The entry is in German and the pertinent portion[63]

---

[60] My underlines.

[61] See above, p. 177.

[62] The entry appears just before the book's index.

[63] "Wir unten benanten aus unserer Evangelische Lutherische Religion, welche Doctor Martin Luther 1530 vor dem gantzen reich zu Augspurg öffentlich bekant. Dahero auch diese Lehre die ungeEnderte Augspurgische Confession genannet wird zu welche Symbole oder glaubens bekentnus wiert uns Ein müstig [unmüs-

179

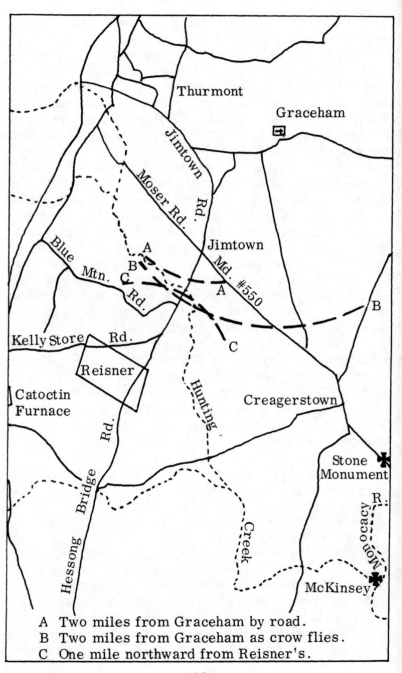

A Two miles from Graceham by road.
B Two miles from Graceham as crow flies.
C One mile northward from Reisner's.

may be translated thus: "We, named below,[64] of our Evangelical Lutheran Religion, which Doctor Martin Luther in the year 1530 publicly confessed at Augsburg before the entire empire and which is therefore called the Unaltered Augsburg Confession,[65] to which symbol or belief we also freely confess, this above-mentioned congregation built the Evangelical Lutheran church a little mile northward from Michael Reisner's plantation in the time of Pastor David Candler as is reckoned one thousand seven hundred forty-three after the gracious birth of our Saviour and Spiritual Maker, Jesus Christ...."[66]

---

sig] bekennen Diese oben gemelte gemein bauete die Evangelische Lutherische Kirch Eine kleine meil Von michael reisner seiner Plantation, Nort werts zur Zeit des Herrn Pfarrherrns David Candlers, als mann zehlte Ein Tausent sieben Hundert Drey und Vierzig nach der Gnaden reichen geburt unsers Heÿlandes und seeligmachers Jesu Christi in dieser gemelte Kirch mit nahmen...."

[64] No names are appended to the Church Book copy.

[65] Pastor Näsman's knowledge of Lutheran history was somewhat inaccurate: Melanchthon, not Luther, compiled the Confession which he "presented" to Emperor Charles V at the Diet of Augsburg. Luther's break with Rome had occurred in 1521 at the Diet of Worms.

[66] This document also includes additional argument against the existence of a town of Monocacy. In referring to the 1743 Monocacy church and its successor church in the town of Frederick, which had just been built, the document later distinguishes between them thus (my underlines): "....our Evangelical Lutheran congregation who have built the above-mentioned church in the hills and the church in the new city of Friederichs Tawn...." ("....aus unserer Evangelische Lutherische gemein welche die oben gemelte Kirch am Geburge und die Kirch in der Neuen Stadt Friederichs Tawn....").

Again with thanks to the work done by the Traceys, we are able to locate Michael Reisner's plantation in terms of today's geography. Known then as GREEN SPRING, it straddled today's Hessong Bridge Road and extended northwesterly. Except for its northernmost corner, it lay south of the Kelly Store Road.

The question now arises, from what part of Reisner's plantation should one measure the "little mile northward"? More significantly, on whose land could the Lutheran church have been located?

Based on all the information available to me, I think it makes relatively little difference where we begin to measure that little mile. In my opinion, its terminus must lie in one place only: on a parcel called SMITH'S LOT, which was also the property of Michael Reisner!

SMITH'S LOT was granted to Reisner on February 6, 1743 for 50 acres, although in the survey of SUGAR CAMP, made on June 1, 1814,[67] it is shown to have contained only $43\frac{3}{4}$ acres clear of other surveys. The beginning point of SMITH'S LOT is indicated in the 1814 survey, and by reference to that survey and to an 1848 deed from Martin Eichelberger to John and Samuel Eicholtz,[68] wherein the beginning point is described as being at the end of the deed's sixth course, this point can be located on today's Frederick County Tax Map.

Beginning at that point, I have platted SMITH'S LOT on, and to the scale of, the Tax Map (see pp. 184-185). This platting places SMITH'S LOT with its eastern part within land now owned by George C. Zinkham, Jr., and the balance on the farm of Wilmer A. Ullmann to the southwest.

Such a location was not only a mile northward from Reisner's home plantation on GREEN SPRING. It was

---

[67] Frederick County Unpatented Certificate of Survey #838.
[68] Frederick County Land Records, ES9-118.

also two miles from Graceham. The distances seem most corroborative.

Reisner sold SMITH'S LOT to John Bytsell (Bytle) on August 1, 1747. In the deed, the beginning point of SMITH'S LOT was described as "a bounded white oak tree standing on the west side of a branch of Grate [sic] Hunting Creek."[69] The courses and distances are not significantly different from those in the 1814 survey except for overlaps discovered by the latter.

For all his somewhat violent way of life, Michael Reisner was definitely an important man in the first Lutheran church. It would have been most logical, therefore, for him to permit the church to be built on his small tract of 50 acres rather than clutter his larger plantation with it. In fact, there may have been more than mere coincidence that he acquired possession of SMITH'S LOT very early in the same year the church was built and that he disposed of it about the time the Lutherans were erecting their successor church in Frederick Town.

There was a large tract of land between GREEN SPRING and SMITH'S LOT. Apparently Charles Carroll, barrister, had some claim on this, but it was not surveyed in his name until 1763 when it was called FIRST DIVIDEND.[70] If Carroll, a Catholic, had such a claim, a Lutheran congregation could scarcely expect to build its church there. And if it was vacant, it would have been very impolitic to put a church on such land.

North of SMITH'S LOT the land was owned mostly by Jacob Weller. Between 1738 and 1753 he acquired

---

[69] Prince George's County Land Records, EE-273. The original courses were: N4°W 30 perches, S50°W 68 perches, N53°W 54 perches, S38°W 88 perches, S33°E 54 perches and a straight line to the beginning, for 50 acres.

[70] Frederick County Patented Certificate of Survey, #1388.

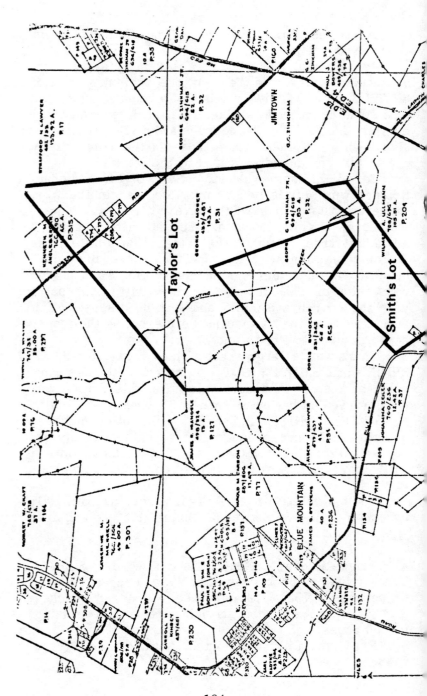

Taylor's Lot

Smith's Lot

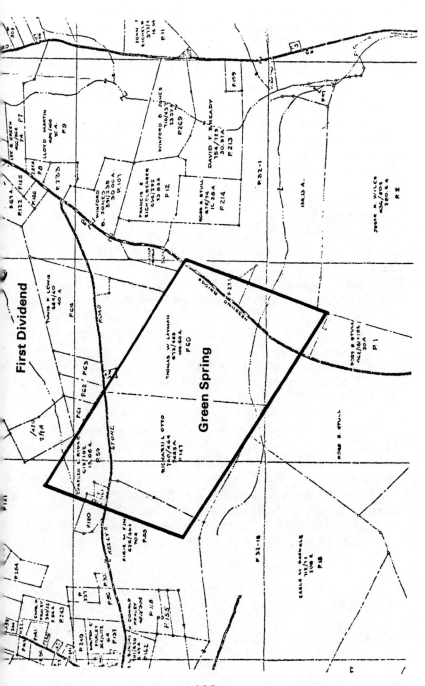

more than 500 acres in the vicinity, some of it so close that 1⅜ acres of SMITH'S LOT were ultimately found to lie foul on Weller's TAYLOR'S LOT.[71] Eventually the Weller family held land all along the northern boundary of FIRST DIVIDEND, i.e., north and west of GREEN SPRING, and finally came into possession of even SMITH'S LOT itself.

From our knowledge of the Lutherans' closing of their church to the Moravians, whose lay leader was this very same Jacob Weller, and his throwing both his home and his land open to the Moravians until Graceham could be begun, it becomes inconceivable that the Monocacy Lutheran Church could have been located on his land!

Aside from what I have been saying about the logic of placing the church on Reisner's SMITH'S LOT, there is strong support for this in the church records. The first paragraph of the church constitution which Muhlenberg wrote in the church book in June 1747 has been quoted above.[72]

In this very first paragraph, Muhlenberg was undoubtedly undertaking to limit ownership of the church building to Lutheran congregations. He was painfully aware of the growing conflict between his orthodox Lutherans and those who were either already Moravians or inclined that way. Since no legal title to the church site has ever been found — and probably never existed — Muhlenberg could impose such limitations only because the site was the property of one of his faithful members. In view of what we know concerning land ownership in the area, that member could have been none other than Michael Reisner.

I have walked the land with Mr. Zinkham and stood with him beside the pile of stones which he identifies

---

[71] Cf. SUGAR CAMP, Frederick County Unpatented Certificate of Survey #838, 1814. Cf. also pp. 184-185.
[72] Cf. p. 177, note 54.

as marking the beginning corner of SMITH'S LOT. The white oak tree is long gone, but the stone pile is "on the west side of a branch of....Hunting Creek." This corner was formerly in the property line between that of George C. Zinkham, Sr., and Anderson Eicholtz. The corner was once mildly in dispute, and hence is known both to Mr. Zinkham, Jr., and to members of the Eicholtz family.

With a compass we traced the eastern boundary of SMITH'S LOT, estimating its length since we had no surveyor's chain. That boundary follows the small branch which flows perhaps 100 feet to the east of it, and the land is level and free of marshland — an ideal building site. All of this makes it logical to assume that the church was built along the eastern border of SMITH'S LOT.

Obviously we searched for any vestige of the church site — but obviously, also, with no hope of success. The log church has been too long abandoned to leave any trace of its existence. Quite possibly the change of land ownership occasioned by Reisner's sale of SMITH'S LOT to Bytsell in 1747 materially shortened the life of the little church.

While there is no definite date of its abandonment known, Dr. Wentz states, "In 1749 it is recorded that all these things (the communion utensils) are in the hands of George Michael Jesserang, and five months later they are committed to Jacob Bene. Thus they have reached the town (church)...."[74] Six years after it was built, the log church "in the hills" was already on its way to oblivion!

---

[73] Wentz, op. cit., p. 121.

INDEX

Place Names are in Frederick County, Maryland unless otherwise indicated.

189

195

Maryland State Highways:
#26: 150-151
#71: 167
#80: 17
#85 (see also Great Road): 15, 17
#180 (Frederick Rd. from Jefferson): 56, 58, 69, 120, 124, 134-136
#194: 153-156, 167
#355: 71
#464: 131, 159
#550 (Jimtown): viii, 175, 180, 184
Masonry 44-45
Matlock, T. Chalkley 17
"Matthew's Good Will" 60, 62, 106, 127-129, 131, 134-135
"Matthew's Lott" 12
Matthews, George 130
Matthews, William 7, 10-11, 64
Matthias, Jacob 175
May, Mary Hershperger 29, 31
Medley, Mrs. Eleanor 19-21, 23-25, 27
Medley Election District 20
Melanchthon, Philipp 181
Mercer, Perry G. 44
Mercersburg, Penna. 123
"Meredith's Hunting Quarters" 69
Methodist Episcopal Churches:
Jefferson 40-41, 51
Walkersville 153, 156
Methodist Protestant Church:
Jefferson 34, 44
Michael, Andrew 48
Middle Alley, Frederick 85
Middle District, Frederick County 107
Middletown vii, 4, 18-19, 22, 47, 94, 98, 115, 120-121, 123-124, 137-148
Fire Engine Lottery 148
Jefferson Street 148
Lutheran Cemetery 121
Lutheran Church 94, 103, 146, 148
Lutheran Church Book 103
Lutheran "Parson's House" 148
Reformed Cemetery 120-121, 123
Reformed Church, German 94
Seminary of English Learning 145
Washington Street 148
Middletown Road (from Jefferson), Old 4, 21-22, 26-27, 32, 38-39, 41, 48, 56, 58, 134
Middletown Valley vii, 87, 106, 128
Mifflin, Thomas 78
Mill Creek (see also Little Catoctin Creek) 82, 113
"Mill Seat Secured," The 54
Miller, Abraham 176
Mills vii, 53-55, 57
Miller, Frederick 147
Missouri 81, 87
Monocacy Church, Lutheran: see Churches
"Monocacy Manor" 98, 149-152, 154-155, 169
Monocacy Quakers: see Quakers, Monocacy
Monocacy Region 170-178
Monocacy River vii, 6, 15, 55, 57-58, 69, 98, 117, 136, 149, 151-152, 154, 163-166, 168-171, 176, 180

Monocacy Road, German 164
Monocacy town or village vii, 157, 161-164, 166-169, 173, 181
Montgomery County 11, 13, 20, 49-50, 158
Moore, Ada 11
Moravians 174-175, 177-178, 186
Moser Road viii, 175, 180, 184
Motter, Valentine 146, 148
"Mount Hope" 12, 14
Mount Olive Cemetery, Frederick 123
Mount Pleasant 171-172
Mount Pleasant Election District 152
Mount Zion Cemetery near Lucas, Ohio 120-121
Mount Zion Lutheran Church, Feagaville 69-70
Mountville Road 56
Mouth of Monocacy 55, 57-58, 69, 136
Muhlenberg, Henry Melchior 167, 173-179, 186
Mulberry Grove, Charles County 66
Müller, Anna Maria (Magdalena): see Culler, Anna Maria (Magdalena) Müller
Müller, Elizabeth: see Culler, Elizabeth Müller
Müller, Jacob 83
Müller, Maria 84
Munch, Orie 100-101
Murry, Mrs. 23, 38
Myers, Caspar 118
Myers, Melissa C. 162
"Myers Addition" 82, 88
Myersville 5, 82, 98, 114-115
Myersville-Middletown Road 115
Näsman, Gabriel 173-174, 179, 181
National Archives, Washington 110
Nead, Dr. D. W. 162
Neale, Bennett 20, 24-26
Neale, Charles 24-25
Neale, Elizabeth Sprigg 26
Neale, James 145
Negroes 41-42
"Neighbors Alarmed" 60, 62
Nelson, John 133
Nelson Family 160
New Freedom vii, 4-5, 18, 31-36, 39, 45-48, 65
Plat of 32-33, 34-35, 46
"New Freedom" tract 4-5, 35, 46, 48, 65
New Garden (Monthly Quaker) Meeting 7, 170
New Jersey 78
New Market 19
New Town (Trap) vii, 18-27, 30-32, 34-36, 39-40, 44, 49, 60, 62, 134, 143, 145
Plat of 21, 26, 35-36
New York State 168
Nicodemus, Frank C. 154
Nicodemus heirs, John D. 153, 155
Ninke (Nieke), Georg 175, 179
Nixdorff, Henry 41
Nollert, Philip 141
North Carolina 61, 77, 87-88
Nyberg, Laurentius 174, 178-179
Nye, Jacob 93
Ohio 79, 81, 88, 107-108, 134